BEYOND THE NEW MORALITY

The Responsibilities of Freedom

Beyond the New Morality

The Responsibilities of Freedom

Revised Edition

GERMAIN GRISEZ
and
RUSSELL SHAW

UNIVERSITY OF NOTRE DAME PRESS
NOTRE DAME   LONDON

Library of Congress Cataloging in Publication Data

Grisez, Germain Gabriel, 1929–
  Beyond the new morality.

  Bibliography: p.
  Includes index.
  1. Ethics.   I.   Shaw, Russell B., joint
author.   II.   Title.
BJ1025.G7   1980   170   80-18293
ISBN 0-268-00663-6
ISBN 0-268-00665-2 (pbk.)

Manufactured in the United States of America

The authors affectionately dedicate
this work to their wives:

Jeannette Grisez
and
Carmen Shaw

Contents

Introduction

[handwritten: A questioning study of right & wrong]

[handwritten: suppost] We are proposing an ethics. But what is *ethics*? As we use the word, it means a philosophical study of morality, of the foundations on which morality is based, and of the practical implications of a systematic moral outlook. *[handwritten: Actual human activity]*

We believe that ethics must start with a clarification of the fundamental notions of freedom, action, and community. Then it can go on to examine the question What is the ultimate distinction between moral good and moral evil, between action which is right and action which is wrong? An answer to this question becomes practically attainable, however, only after one has first worked out a satisfactory way of thinking through concrete moral issues—"Should I do this or that?" "Should I support this or that approach to a public issue?"— and so we next turn to this problem of establishing basic moral principles. Finally, once one is in a position to take a reasoned view of moral issues, one can ask and try to answer the question To what extent is it possible to close the gap, in one's life and in society, between the way one thinks things ought to be and the way they are?

History studies many of the same questions as ethics, but history looks at particular actions which have actually taken place, while ethics is concerned with human action in general or with possible kinds of actions. Psychology and the social sciences also have somewhat the same subject matter as ethics, but psychology and the social sciences are mainly concerned with how human beings actually do act and societies actually do work, while ethics concentrates on how persons ought to act and societies ought to be formed and reformed.

Theological ethics (moral theology or Christian ethics) deals with many of the same questions which are treated here philosophically. The principal difference is that theological ethics takes for granted, as a point of departure, the doctrines of a religious faith, while a philosophical approach does not take for granted any particular set of beliefs. Although it is impossible to question everything at once, the philosophical approach regards every belief and viewpoint as in principle subject to questioning.

In trying to answer the questions which it asks, philosophy points to facts which anyone can observe and proposes arguments which any reasonable person should accept. The nature of the questions it asks causes philosophy to appeal more to arguments than to empirical, concrete facts. "Arguments" here does not mean contentious disagreements, however. Ethics argues mainly in the sense that it proposes clarifications of the meaning of certain basic notions, such as "doing an act" and "morally good," and then draws out implications of these basic notions.

1. The Roots of the Ethical Problem

The central problems of ethics present themselves to a philosopher today in a historical context. Here we cannot go into that context in detail, but it is necessary at least to indicate the deep historical roots of the ethical problems with which people today continue to grapple.

These roots are twofold. On the one side is the Judeo-Christian religious tradition; on the other, the Greco-Roman humanistic tradition.

The belief that God is the creator of all things is part of the Judeo-Christian religious tradition. And the act of creation is pictured not as an accident, nor as something God had to do, nor as an effort on his part to fulfill some sort of need, but as a completely free act. Also part of this religious tradition is the belief that human beings are made in God's image and somehow possess a freedom resembling the freedom by which God creates.

The Judeo-Christian tradition is based on the belief that God freely reveals himself to humankind and, in doing so, extends to human beings the offer of a special, personal relationship—an offer to which they in turn freely respond. Jews believe they are free to accept or reject the Covenant proposed through Moses; Christians believe they are free to accept or reject the Gospel of Jesus Christ. Of course, both Jew and Christian also believe they ought to accept the Covenant or the Gospel.

Thus, for those in the Judeo-Christian tradition human beings have freedom of self-determination. They can make or break their whole existence by their own acts, their own free choices, just as God was able to create—and could as well not have created—by his own free choice.

When, however, the Bible deals with moral good and moral evil, with what is right and what is wrong, it undertakes no general explanation of these concepts. The Covenant and the Gospel contain specific commands, which are represented as God's will; and the Bible always assumes that acting in accord with divine commands will be in the best interests of human beings. But it makes no extended attempt to explain why this should be so, beyond emphasizing that the well-being of human persons depends upon their friendship with God, their creator.

The Greek philosophical tradition worked out various conceptions of what a human being is. Each of these conceptions of human nature served as the basis for an ideal of human

life. In other words, having developed ideas about what a
human being should be, the Greek philosophers went on to
discuss how individuals should live their lives in order to measure up to the ideal.

Although they disagreed considerably in the details of
their views of ethics, the Greek philosophers did agree on
several points. 1) There must be one ideal pattern of human
life. 2) Rational inquiry should be sufficient to reveal this
ideal. 3) The ideal is rooted in human nature, not in individual preferences or divine commands. 4) Individuals fall
short of the ideal either because of hereditary defects (slaves,
for example, are just naturally inferior), or because of bad
upbringing (children brought up in a barbarian culture can
only be semihuman), or because of lack of knowledge of what
is good.

In short, the Greek philosophers developed quite definite
ideas about what a human being must do to live a good, fully
human life. These ideas were proposed on rational grounds,
as corresponding to the requirements of human nature. But
there was no place in their thinking for the idea of freedom of
self-determination.

Throughout the history of Western culture thinkers have
been trying to join elements from the Judeo-Christian religious tradition and the Greco-Roman philosophical tradition
into one harmonious whole. If one takes from the Judeo-
Christian tradition the idea that human beings have freedom
of self-determination and from the Greco-Roman tradition
the idea that there must be a reasonable basis for judgments
of moral good and evil, right and wrong, one has the parts of
the puzzle which ethics confronts.

Divine commands are not in the picture for ethics, since it
cannot proceed by taking for granted particular religious beliefs. In saying this we are not rejecting religious morality or
denying the possibility that there are moral truths which must
be accepted on the basis of religious faith. We are merely

saying that such moral truths, if they exist and important as they may be, are not part of the concern of philosophical ethics. Similarly, ethics today no longer assumes much of the fixity of human nature which the Greco-Roman philosophic tradition took for granted. Instead, we now take for granted the creative capacity and dignity of the individual person.

An adequate solution to the puzzle of ethics must therefore do full justice to two facts: human beings have freedom of self-determination—they determine what they make of their own lives; and human beings have real moral responsibilities—there can be good reasons for judgments of right and wrong. The solution does not lie in denying human freedom or in treating moral requirements as the result of either arbitrary human preferences or humanly inexplicable divine commands.

2. *Why Ethics Is Important*

All children are brought up according to particular moral viewpoints, conveyed to them as much by actions as by words. Small children take for granted the rightness of the morality in which they are being raised; they may not always obey it, but it does not even occur to them to deny its reality and validity. At some point in adolescence or youth, however, most people in our culture become aware that it is open to them to keep, amend, or even replace the moral outlook in which they were raised.

These options are extremely important. Here the framework of one's whole life is at stake. It is unfortunate if, as sometimes happens, so basic a decision is made whimsically, or simply in rebellion against the viewpoint in which one was raised, or merely by conforming to the predjudices of one's class and age group. A person's basic moral stance should be the subject of his or her most careful inquiry and most critical judgment.

The study of ethics provides an opportunity for such careful inquiry and critical judgment. If one is to avoid turning one's life over blindly to the old morality or the new morality, or to the opinions of friends or the demands of feelings, it is necessary to think things through. The only way to do this properly is to do it for oneself and from the ground up.

This book is not a substitute for such personal thinking. The viewpoint which it advances is proposed as one alternative—among many—to be considered seriously. We think it deserves consideration; it is the outcome of our personal inquiry and reflection, and we are convinced of its soundness. But we do not ask anyone to believe what we say; we ask only that the reader examine the questions discussed here and consider the reasons given for the views which are expressed.

People with deep, personal religious faith may feel that it is not necessary for them to undertake the sort of reflection in depth which we are proposing—that they already have an altogether satisfactory moral framework for their lives and need look no further into the questions with which philosophical ethics is concerned. We cannot agree with this point of view, even if the religious faith in question should happen to be one we share. Religious persons need not reduce everything they believe to reasons, but they do need to assure themselves that their act of faith is itself morally defensible in human terms. Furthermore, one can hardly think out a sound theological ethics unless one has worked through the problems the philosopher must face.

The study of ethics has, moreover, an importance which goes beyond the individual and his or her personal life. We live in a society which is pluralistic, a society in which there are disagreements about basic issues. When we find ourselves at odds with our fellow citizens on matters of public policy, we cannot rest on an appeal to beliefs which they do not share.

In this context we must be ready to give good reasons for our judgments about right and wrong.

Only by thinking through our own fundamental outlook are we in a position to articulate the strongest possible case for our judgments. Of course, it is altogether possible—even probable—that even if we understand ourselves, we shall be unable to convince others by philosophic arguments alone. But where fundamental issues are at stake, it is worth the effort to try. For what is the alternative? Propaganda, which is a kind of violence to reason. And when the universal use of propaganda renders all propaganda ineffective, the final "argument" becomes coercion and outright physical violence.

People who care for others and respect themselves do not want to use violence to back up their views. Thus, even if ethical reflection does not seem very likely to lead to agreement in a pluralistic society, it is worth trying. The fact that one falls short of total success does not necessarily mean that nothing has been accomplished. In our society many disputes are settled by means of compromise short of violence and without fundamental agreement. To negotiate the compromises most acceptable to our own convictions, we need to understand our own positions and our reasons for them.

Thus ethics has a vital role to play in our individual lives, by making it possible for us really to take possession of ourselves; and it also has an important place in our lives as members of a pluralistic society.

3. The Nature of This Book

It will be clear to any reader, and especially to professional philosophers, that this is not a technical work of philosophy. That is not said defensively, but only as a caveat to those who might otherwise approach the book expecting what it does

BEYOND THE NEW MORALITY

not pretend to offer. One of the authors, Grisez, has set forth
his ethical theory at length and in the language of technical
philosophy in other publications and will probably continue
to do so in the future. Professionals in the field are urged to
consult these expositions for a statement of the theory and
examples of its application, in terms to which they are accus-
tomed.

For whom is this book intended? The primary audience is
the ethics class, where a teacher can supplement the book's
presentation with the degree of technical and professional
sophistication he or she deems appropriate. In the authors'
minds, however, the audience is by no means limited to students in formal classes. Others, such as adult study and discussion groups, will find it useful. It is also the authors' hope
that the serious reader, reading independently, will study and
reflect on it.

The present work does not attempt to set forth a variety of
views; it is not a history of ethics or an overview of the field.
Rather, it seeks to state clearly and simply, in language com-
prehensible to the nonprofessional, a particular approach to
ethics. For this reason it may well be read in conjunction with
other works which propose other approaches.

For all audiences the "questions for review and discussion"
after each chapter and the list of readings at the end of the
book provide an additional dimension. The questions are not
meant to catechize readers but to encourage them to engage
in further exploration of the issues raised and further evaluation of the answers offered here (as well as other answers
offered by other ethical systems). As for the readings, they do
not comprise a comprehensive bibliography of ethics since
such bibliographies are readily available elsewhere. Instead
they identify two kinds of sources: those which complement
and/or develop at greater length particular points made in the
text and those which illustrate points of view with which the
theory proposed takes issue.

4. The Plan of the Book

The best way to determine how the argument is developed is, naturally, to read the book. What follows is meant only as a brief look ahead for those who may wish such assistance.

We begin with freedom, since the question of moral good and moral evil involves the question of freedom—how it is used or abused. Freedom, however, cannot be understood apart from action; and our analysis distinguishes three separate levels of action, with a particular "freedom" associated with each. Our principal concern is with the third level of action (self-determination) and its corresponding freedom, since it is at this level that one can speak most properly of moral good and moral evil. We note, further, that the individual as a moral entity does not exist in isolation: relationships with other people are part of the fabric of life, and ethics must therefore deal with the community dimension of living.

All this, however, is only groundwork for identifying principles by which one can determine whether an action is morally good or morally evil. Rejecting the solutions of relativism and subjectivism, we argue that the fundamental criterion is the manner in which one makes free, self-determining choices. In chapter nine we identify two ways of choosing—one open to goods not chosen, the other not open—and conclude that the former is morally good because it leaves one open to continuing and ever-greater growth as a person.

Next we move to the identification of guidelines which help people to choose rightly. First utilitarianism is rejected, because it locks one into an immoral pattern of choice. Instead, eight "modes of responsibility" are identified (in chapters eleven through thirteen) as guidelines for choosing as well as for analyzing action. The problem of "ambiguous" action is examined in chapter fourteen, and a solution proposed in terms of the modes of responsibility.

The final section of the book applies what has gone before to several matters of particular concern, such as education, social reform and revolution, and theories of individual and social progress. The special role of religion in regard to morality (Is it a help or a hindrance?) is considered at some length. The book ends with a brief description of how persons who wish to do what is morally right might structure their lives.

It will be apparent at many points that this book is concerned in a special way with the "new morality." The new morality means different things to different people, but the general idea is that traditional morality placed too much emphasis on inflexible general rules, on obedience, and on abstract ideals of right and wrong; whereas the emphasis of the new morality is on the concrete situation, on love, and on the person.

On the whole we are sympathetic to the intentions of proponents of the new morality. But we are not satisfied with the positions they have worked out. We do not suggest a return to the old morality; that is in any case no longer possible. Rather, we suggest an advance beyond the new morality toward a sounder and more humane ethics. The new morality is only a halfway house.

The ethics we propose here takes full account of the concrete situation, of love, and of the person. But it also seeks to put the concrete situation into the context of the whole of a person's life; it seeks to show how love requires a free response to human goods, a response which generates responsibilities; it seeks to defend the person and the community of persons against the implications of theories and attitudes that would make of them mere objects, mere means.

*   *   *   *   *

A work resulting from collaboration naturally raises questions in readers' minds. Who is responsible for which ideas?

Who wrote what? Does the book reflect thoroughgoing agreement or a series of compromises?

One of the authors of this book, Grisez, is a professional philosopher; the other, Shaw, is a professional writer. The ethical theory set forth here is, properly speaking, Grisez's. The authors have, however, discussed ethics with each other frequently and have arrived at a substantial harmony of view. In addition, they have worked together on several writing projects involving ethics besides this one.

The book came about in the following way. Grisez's ethics course for an entire semester was recorded and transcribed. Grisez also drew up an outline of a short book on ethics— more or less this book. Working from the transcript and the outline while retaining considerable independence as to the ordering of the material and the manner of stating and illustrating concepts, Shaw produced a manuscript. The authors conferred and revised, added and subtracted. The result was the first edition of this book, published in 1974. In preparing the second edition a less exhaustive but similarly collaborative process of discussion and revision was employed. In addition, the authors took into account—and here gratefully acknowledge—reactions and criticisms of teachers, students, and other readers who worked with the first edition.

The result is *Beyond the New Morality* as it now stands. The authors regard it as a joint enterprise, for which they are willing to share not only blame but (they continue to hope) also praise.

1: Freedom Means Responsibility

Freedom. Everybody wants it. Poets praise it. Politicians promise or proclaim it. Some people have given their lives to win it for themselves or others.

But what is it?

The word "freedom" can have many different meanings. It can refer simply to the lack of physical restraints. It can mean the absence of external social pressures and demands. And it can signify that state in which individuals are able to form their own lives—in a sense, their own *selves*—through their choices.

It makes a difference what kind of freedom one is talking about. True, there are common elements: for example, as applied to persons, the meaning of freedom includes at least someone acting, the activity, and something else—a factor potentially in opposition to the activity. Common elements aside, however, the various meanings of freedom are significantly different. Furthermore, the freedom to determine one's self by one's own choices is the freedom most proper to a human being. It is the freedom with which ethics is most concerned.

Because there are different kinds of freedom, and because some are more properly human than others, it is worth looking at them in some detail in order to see where they are different and in what each consists.

1

1. Freedom Is Physical Freedom

The simplest kind of freedom is the absence of physical coercion and constraint. This is what is called physical freedom. Even inanimate objects can have it: we speak, for example, of "freely falling bodies." It is also the kind of freedom enjoyed typically by wild animals, in contrast with those in captivity, and by infants. On the other hand, a prisoner in a cell does not have freedom in this sense (or else possesses it only to a limited degree and in a highly circumscribed way) because he is physically prevented from doing many things, including leaving the cell. Someone forced to perform a physical action, or physically prevented from doing so, is not acting freely in performing or not performing the action.

Physical freedom corresponds to the simplest kind of action, that which can be performed even by an animal or an infant. A dog chases a rabbit. A baby crawls across a room to get a red ball. In such action the meaning of the behavior comes from its culmination. And the behavior and the meaning are closely united. The behavior only makes sense in terms of the culminating performance (catching the rabbit, getting the ball).

Freedom is present in such action only in the sense that the behavior cannot take place unless the individual is not physically constrained. Where there is constraint, there can be no action; where there is no constraint, the action can be performed. The latter situation represents physical freedom.

This kind of freedom is always a matter of degree. Some measure of physical freedom is essential if one is to act morally. (Acting morally here does not mean doing what is right. It only means acting in a way that *counts* as right or wrong in moral terms.) At the same time, however, absolute physical freedom is not required for moral responsibility. In fact, it is nonsense to speak of "absolute physical freedom." Everyone is subject to some constraint—the law of gravity would see to that if nothing else did. Freedom in the sense of physical freedom is always more or less.

2. *Freedom Is Doing As One Pleases*

Freedom can also mean doing as one pleases because of the absence of social demands and restrictions. A slave's basic condition is not one of freedom in this sense, because what the slave does and does not do is determined by someone else, his or her master. (Slaves may also be deprived of physical freedom, though this need not be the case.) By contrast, Robinson Crusoe was totally free to do as he pleased until Friday appeared on the scene to inject social obligations to another. Since there was until then no one else to impose societal demands and restrictions on Crusoe, he enjoyed complete freedom to do as he pleased.

As is the case with physical freedom, so freedom to do as one pleases corresponds to a particular sort of action. This kind of freedom is proper to action performed as a means to some end which is separate from the performance itself, an end not included in the culmination of the behavior. An example of this kind of action is planting seed in order to obtain a crop. Obtaining the crop is the end which is sought, but it is very widely separated, not only in time but in other ways as well, from the performance of sowing seed.

At this level of action persons are free to do as they please to the extent that they desire the end to be achieved and that certain means are necessary to achieve the end. The grain-crop example clearly meets the second condition because there will be no crop unless the seed is planted; as for the first—desiring the end—it is fulfilled in the case of a farmer who plants seed because he wants a crop; it is not fulfilled in the case of a slave who plants seed only because his master tells him to.

Several things are characteristic of action at this level. Calculation—reflection on what means to employ in order to achieve particular ends—is both possible and necessary. Also, it is clear that at this level doing as one pleases and responsibility are in opposition to each other. Responsibility in society is something which is imposed on one by other people. Freedom to do as one pleases lies in the absence of such imposition. Individuals would be totally free at this level of action if they had to do only those things necessary to achieve the ends *they* wanted to achieve.

Immature people tend to think that this is the highest kind of freedom. Adolescents seeking to shake off the requirements imposed on them by authority typically are seeking freedom of this sort. Doing what one pleases appears to be the very highest expression of what freedom is, and this is the opposite of doing as one is required by parents, teachers, or others in authority. A more mature view of the matter, however, suggests that merely doing as one pleases is neither the final word on freedom nor an unqualified good.

Some degree of freedom to do as one pleases is certainly essential to moral responsibility. However, unlimited freedom of this sort is impossible—and would be undesirable even if it were somehow not impossible—for anyone living in social relationships with others. If people did not have real responsibilities to one another, if all went their own ways and acted without concern for others, society would collapse.

More important than unrestricted freedom to do as one pleases is that individuals be able to participate in appropriate ways in setting up and directing their relationships and the communities which make demands and place restrictions on them. People have a right to a voice in setting the rules of the societies in which they live. But this is a very different thing from, practically speaking, opting out of societies and the demands they make in order to have maximum freedom to do as one pleases.

3. *Ideal Freedom, Creative Freedom, and Political Freedom*

Before passing on to the kind of freedom most important to ethics, it is worth mentioning several other kinds of freedom: ideal freedom, creative freedom, and freedom in the political sense.

"Ideal freedom" refers to the freedom possessed by individuals and societies which are able to act in accord with an ideal. This is the sense in which the word "freedom" is used by such different thinkers as St. Paul and Freud.

St. Paul considered the sinner not to be free because, on account of sin, he or she is bound to fall short of the ideal of uprightness. By contrast, he held Christians to be free because their redemption from sin by Christ freed them for uprightness. Similarly, for Freud the neurotic is not free; but the cured patient, who has been liberated from neurosis, is to that extent free to behave in accord with an ideal of psychological health.

Ideal freedom and freedom to do as one pleases may sound at first like complete opposites—shaping one's actions to conform to an ideal as against acting without constraint—but they can be compatible. Ideal freedom means that the individual is not blocked from doing what ought to be done; freedom to do as one pleases means that the individual is not blocked from doing as he or she wishes to do. But underlying most ideals of behavior is the assumption that, once reached, they will be found easy and pleasant to fulfill, and people will actually wish to do so.

In practice the content of ideal freedom varies widely. There are diverse conceptions of the ideal condition of the human agent and diverse views of the obstacles to the fulfillment of the ideals. Marx, for example, considered the ideal human condition to be attainable not by isolated individuals but only by society as a whole. Yet whatever the particular content, the general concept remains the same: human beings will have ideal freedom when they can act as they ideally ought to do. And if one's ideal for human beings includes their realizing themselves by their own free choices, then ideal freedom will be closely related to the most important sort of freedom, freedom of self-determination, to be discussed below.

"Creative freedom" refers to the freedom present when circumstances and factors which tend toward repetition are overcome and that which is new emerges. This is the freedom peculiar, for example, to a creative artist, inasmuch as the artist does not merely repeat what has been done before but creates a work possessing an element of genuine newness. Some philosophers have gone so far as to liken the whole of reality to the creative process of art, seeing reality as an ongoing process in which there regularly emerge novelties which are not attributable to antecedent conditions and laws.

Freedom in this sense is distinguishable from physical freedom, since the latter resides in the agent engaging in a behavior, whereas creative freedom can involve the emergence of something new and distinct from the agent. Creative freedom is also different from freedom to do as one pleases: the latter can be as repetitive and noncreative as the desires which shape the content of what "one pleases," but new desires can be part of freedom as the emergence of novelty. Finally, creative freedom is not the same as ideal freedom, for the latter takes for granted the prior existence of an ideal of behavior, while creative freedom can involve the emergence of novel ideals and principles.

"Political freedom" suggests a kind of freedom to do as one pleases which applies to peoples rather than to individuals. In this sense a colony revolts and fights for its freedom.

There is, however, another sense of political freedom: namely, the participation of individuals in directing their own polity, which we mentioned at the end of the previous section.

This concept is best expressed by the phrase "government by the consent of the governed."

Although political freedom in this sense is closely related to individual freedom to do as one pleases, the two things are not identical. The difference is one of emphasis. In individual freedom to do as one pleases, the emphasis is on the absence of requirements set by others. In political freedom the emphasis is on the fact that persons act according to laws which they somehow share in making. In this sense children in a typical Western democracy are not politically free, but virtually all adult citizens are. In addition, political freedom is concerned, not with the whole of one's life, but only with the part of it in which one acts as a citizen.

4. Freedom Is Self-determination

As we have suggested, freedom also refers to self-determination—the shaping of one's life, one's *self*, by one's choices. This is the kind of freedom most closely related to questions of morality. To the extent that we can determine for ourselves who we shall be, we are responsible for our lives.

This kind of freedom does *not* assume or require the absence of all external pressures and prior causes. Self-determination refers instead to the state of affairs in which, despite external pressures and prior causes which can and do influence our choices, we retain at least some options of choosing or not choosing, of choosing one thing rather than another.

In cases where there is no such option, there is no real choice and no self-determination. In such cases it is not a question of "moral" action at all. When people do things without really having chosen to do them, they are not acting either morally or immorally; their action simply has no moral quality in itself (although it may be that they have considerable moral responsibility for previous freely chosen acts by which they placed themselves in the position of being unable to choose freely).

It is certainly possible for people to act in this way—without choosing to act—and in fact they often do. But it is also possible for people to act on the basis of real choice and, in doing so, to be self-determining.

Like physical freedom and freedom to do as one pleases, self-determination corresponds to a particular kind of action. At this third level, action derives its meaning from a good in which one participates by performing the action. The meaning does not come from the consummation of the action (first level: physical freedom) nor from a specific goal which the action is meant to achieve (second level: freedom to do as one pleases). Instead the meaning comes from a purpose in which one participates precisely through performing the action. This purpose or good is not achieved at the end of the action or sometime after it but is present in the performance throughout, at every stage; and one realizes a good by participating in it.

Consider an example: studying simply for the sake of learning. Studying is the action. Learning is the purpose or good. Learning is not something which occurs or is achieved only at the end of studying. It goes on all the time one is studying. One participates in this good for as long as one performs the action.

From this same example it is apparent how one and the same action can, simply by a change of perspective—or, more accurately, a change of intention—move from one level to another.

First all actions, even the most complex, can be broken down into their individual first-level components. In studying—reading a chapter in a book, for instance—the eyes move from one line of print to another, and from one page to the next. This simple process of looking at words on a page is activity at the first level of action.

The same act of studying can also be an action at either the second or the third level. It will be an action at the second level if one is studying simply as a means to an end: for example, to pass an examination. But it will be an action of the third level if it is done not merely to achieve an ulterior objective (passing a test) but for the sake of participating in a good (learning) which is intimately and inextricably linked to the action itself. Furthermore, as the example makes clear, the same act can simultaneously be an action at the second level and at the third level—if, for instance, while studying for an exam, one is also learning for learning's sake and is concerned about both purposes at the same time.

5. Determinism

Some theories of human behavior, which go by the general name "determinism," hold that there is really no such thing as freedom of self-determination. They argue that all behavior is determined by factors prior to choice. Many philosophers of the past three centuries, and especially of the nineteenth century, considered belief in self-determination unscientific. They thought that a free choice would violate the physical laws articulated by Newton. Determinists in the English-speaking tradition have generally been identified with what is called "soft determinism" or "compatibilism." In this view human acts can be attributed to the person who performs them, inasmuch as he or she is not coerced, yet the acts are determined by a cause and are not expressions of self-determination.

Determinism is still influential in sociology and psychology; most compatibilists, in fact, are psychological determinists who hold that people necessarily choose the alternative which seems best to them. However, this way of thinking no longer has much support from contemporary physics and logic.

Basically, determinism comes down to saying that every

action is determined in advance; that everyone has to act as he or she does (for instance, because of psychological makeup) and could not choose to act differently. While we do not consider this to be a true or adequate explanation of human action, it does reflect some perfectly accurate observations about certain aspects of human behavior. For one thing, it is entirely true that antecedent factors play an extremely strong role in much behavior, a stronger role than perhaps many people are ready to admit. Some of what passes for free action is probably not really as free as it seems. Only as we have gained insight into psychological conditioning—how it occurs and how it exerts its influence—have we come to understand this.

The concept of self-determination—freedom at the third level of action—does not mean that action takes place without causes that precede it or that the causes do not have a conditioning influence on the action. But it is important to be clear about what, in the case of free choice, the determining conditions do in fact determine. Essentially they determine two things: first, that there are at least two possibilities; second, that everything required including the motivation for one to choose either (or any) of the possibilities is present.

Prior determining conditions quite commonly exclude a large number of actions which might hypothetically be possibilities but which, concretely, are not possibilities here and now for this individual facing a choice. Many people are so impressed by this that they conclude that antecedent conditions have excluded the possibility of choice itself. This is a typical explanation of criminal acts: they are entirely accounted for by poverty, a bad family life, and similar factors, which have robbed the individual of the capacity for free choice. Without ignoring or denying the powerful role of poverty, family influences, and other such factors in crime, we point out that it cannot be taken for granted that such antecedent conditions, through sharply limiting the options open to an individual, have removed the possibility of free choice itself. Not everything people do is a free, self-determined action; but for the average individual it is possible at least sometimes to perform such actions.

Experience points to the truth of this. If all our actions were determined in advance by antecedent factors, we would not have the experience—often very intense and uncomfortable—of unsettledness and indecision in making a choice; there is no reason for deliberation about actions which are already determined. Furthermore, when people make choices, they do not experience choice as *happening to* them but as something they *do:* "I made up my mind." The experience of choice is an experience of acting, not of undergoing. Determinism has to try to explain away our experience that what we do is really ours to decide.

It is reasonable to take such experience at face value unless one has reason for doing otherwise. In fact, it is only reasonable that the data of experience should be accepted as genuine in the absence of a good reason for rejecting them. The burden of proof rests with determinism.

And, as it happens, determinism does not provide grounds for rejecting the validity of the experience of choosing freely. For determinism is self-defeating. It denies the notion of unconditional obligation, because it holds that all actions which would fulfill unconditional responsibilities are determined by antecedent conditions. Yet at the same time it is impossible to propose determinism as a point of view that ought to be accepted without assuming the existence of at least one unconditional obligation: namely, the obligation of being reasonable enough to accept the arguments proposed for determinism. In claiming that their theory is supported by cogent reasons, determinists are saying that we *ought* to accept it, that we *ought* to concur with their view that the experience of self-determination is an illusion. But it makes no sense for determinists to tell us what we *ought* to do—using "ought" as they must in an unconditional sense—if we have no choice about it anyway.

We are left, then, with the conclusion that determinism, as a self-defeating theory, is unable to supply reasonable grounds for rejecting our experience of choosing in a free, self-determining manner. Rationality instructs us to accept this experience as valid. Sometimes at least we do make free choices and, in making them, exercise our freedom of self-determination.

Questions for Review and Discussion

1. Make up—or find in other sources—examples of the use of the word "freedom" in each of the senses distinguished here.

2. The word "responsibility" has different senses corresponding to three of the senses of the word "freedom": namely, physical freedom, freedom to do as one pleases, and freedom of self-determination. What are these three senses of "responsibility"? (For instance, what is the difference between saying that a pet cat is responsible for the scratches on the table top and saying that persons are responsible for their own lives?)

3. In feeling that we don't want others to boss us around, what kind of freedom is it that we want? *2nd level — to do as we please.*

4. We shall see later that moral responsibility is not just a set of rules to be obeyed. Supposing, however, that *were* all there is to morality, would it be incompatible with freedom of self-determination? *Yes, cause I can break these rules*

5. Many people who hold a determinist position nevertheless insist that we are able to act freely. What do you think they mean by this?→ *There are many diff. sorts of determinism. Ex. Sociological determinist. Aristotle*

6. It has been suggested that the idea that people have freedom of self-determination originated in the Judeo-Christian conception of human beings as made in the image of God. Leaving aside the question of whether you do or don't accept the biblical account, investigate the plausibility of this supposition about the origin of the concept of self-determination.

7. Identify, analyze, and evaluate other arguments for or against freedom of self-determination.

2: Being a Person Is a Lifelong Job

Once again want to discuss freedom of self-determination —

How to be a person

In the last chapter we looked closely at freedom, particularly in order to distinguish freedom in the sense of self-determination from freedom in other senses. Self-determination is at the heart of the matter which concerns us in ethics. Now we are ready to take a closer, longer look at freedom of self-determination: what it is and how it works.

Each person has his or her own, special problems, but there is one problem which is common to every person's life, a problem whose solution gives meaning to life. It is how to be a person.

That is a deceptively simple statement. It says more than it seems to say. There are, after all, false notions about human life which go to the fundamental question of what life is all about. When one says that the problem, the challenge, and the meaning of life lie in being a person, one is also rejecting several contrary views about life.

One of these is that the basic problem shared by all people is how to *remain* persons. Another is that the fundamental challenge is how to *become* persons. The contention here is that it is a question, not of remaining or becoming, but of being.

1. Remaining a Person Is Not the Problem

Nonpersons have a definite, given character. They are not self-determining but determined. To be fully themselves, they need only remain themselves, and they usually have little trouble in doing so. As a writer once remarked, "a rose is a rose is a rose." A rose remains a rose; it is in no danger of becoming a dandelion or a turnip.

The same is true even in the case of nonpersons which are capable of acting and changing. Chemicals act and react; plants grow; animals perform in many different ways. In none of these cases, however, is real choice involved. Even animal behavior, which can be very complex and, as we say, "almost human," is not self-determined action. Instead it is a series of determined processes whose meaning comes from the naturally given consummations to which the behavior leads (action at the first level).

Thus an animal does not enjoy freedom of self-determination. It does not choose how it will act; its "choices" are entirely determined for it by its own instincts, by training, and by other circumstances over which it has no control, so that in a true sense it cannot act other than it does. Nor is an animal self-conscious; it has no self of which to be conscious.

The point is that a nonperson (a rock, a plant, an animal) perfectly fulfills itself by remaining what it is and by undergoing whatever changes happen to befall it. It does just what comes naturally, but since it has no freedom in the moral sense, its actions cannot be called morally "good" or morally "bad," "right" or "wrong."

For persons the situation is very different. For them it is not simply a question of remaining what they are or experiencing change without choice. Doing what comes naturally is not enough, even if it were possible just to relax and simply *be*. Rather, persons face the constant need to make choices and, in doing so, to determine themselves. How to use our freedom of self-determination—how, in other words, to *be persons*—is the challenge which continually confronts us.

2. Becoming a Person Is Not the Problem

The challenge of being a person is, however, by no means the same thing as becoming a person. Persons *are* persons; the question for them is how to be what they already are. If the problem were how to *become* a person, it would mean that personhood was some sort of definite, well-defined goal or objective toward which one could work by action at the second level. But this is not the case. Personhood, as we shall spend much of this book seeing, does not have this character. Moreover, it is something we already possess. We are not working toward the goal of becoming persons; we are instead coping constantly with the difficult but fascinating problem of how to *be persons*.

Clearly it is true that one can become a better person or a worse one. But this is something entirely different from becoming a person. When we say that the question facing us is how to become better persons (or to avoid becoming worse ones), we are saying in effect that the fundamental problem we face is how to be persons. Questions of better and worse, good and bad, are questions of how to be.

Thus personhood is not something we achieve, as if it could be the objective of exclusively second-level action by which one labors in a calculating manner to achieve a well-defined goal. The self-made person is a myth, and a confusing one. The question of how to be a person is never settled once and for all in anybody's life. It is the basic question with which all of us wrestle every day, and all the days, of our lives.

3. The Problem Is How to Be a Person

It requires no effort for a person to remain a person. One cannot do anything else. Nor does a person face the challenge of becoming a person. One cannot very well become what one already is.

But for a person the problem of *how to be what one is* is an engrossing challenge. It is a constant question. It is also a lifelong task. The responsibility cannot be evaded. It involves the continual necessity of making choices. One thing about which we have no choice is the absolute imperative of choosing.

It might be objected that suicide offers a way of evading this responsibility. But this is not the case. Suicide is merely one way of responding to the challenge to be a person. Even if one looks at suicide as a kind of choosing-not-to-choose, as an attempt to return to the uncomplicated existence of that which just *is*, it still remains true that this attempt itself is a choice. (Of course, this is true only of suicide when it is freely chosen; if suicide results from determining causes, then it is not a free choice, and neither is it a human action in the sense of being an action which registers on the moral scale.)

How to be a person is a problem of self-determination. Basically it is a problem which we resolve for ourselves by our choices at the third level of action. It is sometimes supposed that in choosing to do something we are only determining our action, not ourselves. This is not true. When we act at the third level—something we all must do at some time or other—we are not just determining our action; we are determining ourselves. In a real sense we are choosing how we will be persons. We are taking ourselves in hand and shaping ourselves through the exercise of our freedom of self-determination.

As we have seen, actions are of three kinds. At the first level are those whose meaning comes from the natural consummation to which they lead. If the action is performed, it naturally ends—barring some physical mishap—in this particular result. We do not give the action its meaning. The meaning is already there. In acting at this level we are not doing anything essentially different from what an animal or a small child could do. We are not determining ourselves; we are simply remaining the sort of thing we already are.

This is not to suggest, however, that persons can simply act instinctively—at the first and simplest level of action—and thereby absolve themselves of moral responsibility. As we have seen, all actions, including those at the third level, can be broken down into their units, and these units are actions at the first level. (A student engaged in study turns the pages of a book, moves his or her eyes from line to line of print, etc.) But these simple units of action do have moral significance when they are, as it were, the building blocks or the concrete embodiment of action at a higher level. This is not the case with animals and may not be the case with very young children unable to choose freely. But it is inescapably the case for persons who can make choices. Even a decision always to act instinctively would itself have moral significance which would color all the actions performed on the basis of this decision.

At the second level of action we act in order to achieve specific, limited goals which are separate and distinct from the action. The meaning of the action is derived from its goal. (The student in the example studies hard in order to pass an examination; passing the exam gives meaning to the studying.) We are not determining ourselves by acting at this level either. For the meaning of the action is derived from its goal, and the goal is outside oneself. Even if it is something very important to the person performing the action—even if passing this particular examination is going to determine whether the student does or doesn't pass the entire course—it is still external to him or her, it is not an aspect of the person's *self*. Action at this second level does not involve self-determination.

It is, however, not possible to choose to act always or even usually at the second level. Where choice is involved, there has to be some third-level action, some commitment to participate in a good. Even if one sought to orient one's life to the pursuit of limited, specific goals, leaving out as much as possible participation in fundamental values, one would be determining the cast of one's life by doing so. And this would be a sign of a fundamental commitment, a real act of self-determination, which itself would be a third-level action serving as a sort of umbrella for many actions at the second level. Like actions at the first level, actions at this second level also derive their moral significance from their relation to purposes that go beyond the limited objectives of the second-level actions themselves.

4. Self-determination

Self-determination occurs at the third level of action. Here it is no longer a question of action whose meaning comes from the consummation to which it naturally leads; nor is it a question of action whose meaning comes from the specific, definite objective at which it aims. At this level the meaning of the action is derived instead from the purpose or good in which one intends to participate by performing the action. The student in our example studies in order to participate in the good of learning (or, perhaps, in order to pass an examination as part of a complex series of steps on the way to becoming a physician in order—the good in which participation is sought—to work in the service of human life and health). It is at this level that morality properly enters the picture, that the problem and opportunity of being—or failing to be—fully a human person exist.

Notice that at this level of action we speak of "participating" in a good, not "achieving" a good. When we refer to achieving something, we are speaking of a limited, definite objective which we can, in effect, grasp and possess as a result of our activity. In speaking of participating in a good, however, we imply that we never fully realize or exhaust it; we also imply that this participation is not something which occurs only at the end of our activity, and as a result of it, but rather that it takes place all the time we are performing the action.

Technique and precise calculation are possible at the second level of action, where we are concerned with achieving specific objectives, but they are not possible at the third level of action, where it is a question of participating in goods. For example, technique and calculation are necessary and appropriate to study well; random, haphazard study in distracting surroundings and circumstances is not likely to pay off in success on an examination. But there is no way of calculating how to participate in the good of learning, how to make study a worthwhile experience in itself without reference to a payoff for studying well.

In third-level action the goal is indefinite and always extends beyond what is done to achieve participation in it. Unlike the second level of action, where one can calculate what and how much to study in order to pass a certain examination, on the third level it is nonsense to suppose that one can study just so much and then consider oneself to have exhausted all further possibility of participating in the good of learning.

✳ Self-determination is possible only when precise calculation is not: that is, only at the third level of action. When we act in this way, we are truly determining ourselves because we are choosing the purposes which constitute ourselves. As we shall see later, the fundamental human goods involved in third-level action are in fact aspects of the human personality; thus we form our characters by the choices which we make at this level.

Character might be defined as the residue of self-determined actions. When people choose at this level, this is how they *are* until they change their minds: the orientation thus given to one's life remains until it is changed. And it can be changed only by a new act of self-determination. That is why even small actions, if they are third-level ones, are important to character formation. When an action, whether large or small, involves self-determination, it contributes to the formation of character.

This in turn suggests why ethical theories are mistaken which say that in ethical terms it is only the overall orientation of one's life which is important and not individual actions. Certainly the overall orientation of one's life is of crucial importance. But this orientation often comes about, not through a single, isolated, basic act of commitment made in a highly self-conscious way, but through the accumulation of small yet significant acts through which, perhaps without adverting to it very consciously, one establishes commitments and a fundamental orientation; this also is the pattern of action by which people commonly reinforce existing commitments and orientations. Individual, isolated third-level actions involving self-determination do serve to constitute the self, either by reaffirming what is already there or setting one, however tentatively, in a new direction. Every act of self-determination, however "small," is morally important.

This analysis also points to the inadequacy of the theory which says that the morality of actions is determined by the situation. The word "situation" is ambiguous, since it can refer to two different things. One is a set of physical facts—what one might call the "physical situation"—which the individual has not brought about and which is not morally defined since it is open to a variety of possible actions, good and bad.

The other might be called the "moral situation"—the situation created when a particular person encounters a particular physical situation (and in which, presumably, one course of action is objectively better than another). This moral situation is not determined by the physical facts but by what the indi-

vidual brings to the physical situation in the way of preconceptions and prior moral commitments.

An example will help to make this clear. The time is sun-
rise. The place is a downtown street near the railroad station.
Lying unconscious in the gutter is a well-dressed man of middle age. This is the physical situation. The moral situation
only comes into being when some other individual enters on
the scene and is required to make a choice regarding what
action to take.

Let us imagine three different people confronting this
physical situation and making a choice about what to do: first,
a woman rushing to catch a train which will take her to work;
second, a dedicated member of Alcoholics Anonymous; third,
a common thief. It is entirely likely that each will respond
differently: the woman commuter by passing by, the Alcoholics Anonymous member by stopping to help, the thief by
robbing the man. Furthermore, it is entirely possible that each
will feel morally justified in the course of action chosen. After
all, even thieves—to say nothing of people who are "too busy to
get involved"—are capable of rationalizing their behavior in
order to justify themselves in their own eyes.

The point of the example, however, is not to demonstrate
that any course of action is acceptable behavior provided one
can find some subjective rationalization for it. Quite the contrary. There is little doubt that in the example given only the
second course of action—stopping to help the fallen man—is,
objectively speaking, the morally right thing to do. But that is
not the point either.

The point instead is that each of these three persons—the
commuter, the Alcoholics Anonymous member, and the
thief—encounters the same physical situation but creates a
different moral situation because of preexisting attitudes and
commitments. It might be said, for example, that the thief's
basic moral commitment (which is a highly immoral one) is to
self-satisfaction. But because this is so, he simply does not see
the physical facts—an unconscious person lying in the

street—in the same way as someone with a different moral commitment. Rather, he perceives this physical situation as one more opportunity for the exercise of his habit of thievery.

In short, the physical situation does not determine the moral situation. Instead, the moral situation is only brought into being by the perceptions and precommitments of the individual. Each person creates his or her own moral situations—although certainly not physical situations—on the basis of self-determination.

Lastly, it is appropriate to note that life has more meaning when one sees the good which is involved in the present situation and acts for the sake of participating in that good. Some acts which are, from one point of view, second-level actions can, by a change of intention, become actions at the third level. In the example of studying, at the second level one studies in order to pass an exam, whereas at the third level one studies in order, say, to learn for the sake of learning itself.

Lest all this sound moralistic with respect to third-level action, we hasten to point out that it is precisely at this level that one can be guilty of moral evil as well as moral good; that efficient, well-planned action at the second level is a necessary, important, and in itself commendable element of human life; and that, as we have already remarked, one seldom if ever acts *only* at the second level but almost always performs actions which partake in some way of third-level commitment.

Nevertheless, it is fair to say that a person who is concentrating on acting at the second level is, to that extent, necessarily looking to the future—to an objective which is to be achieved by the action—whereas a person acting at the third level is living meaningfully in the present, participating here and now in a good through the action which is being performed. And there is a certain absurdity in habitually concentrating on the second-level aspect of what one does—always focusing on future objectives. This robs life of its present meaning, because it situates meaning in something which is always yet to come rather than in something now present in which one is at this moment participating.

The point is not that one should always make the best of any situation, however bad. There are some situations one should bend every effort to change. We are, however, talking about deriving the most meaning from one's present action, whatever it may be. Action has more meaning—more content, one might say—when it is action at the third level.

And just as habitually acting at the third level gives more meaning to life, so it also gives more meaning to death. A person who habitually acts at the third level, the level of self-determination, has participated in human goods throughout the course of life. Such a person's life is a meaningful one at no matter what point it happens to end. By contrast, the life of one who habitually gives preeminence to the second-level aspect of action, emphasizing limited objectives and paying little attention to the challenge and opportunity of participating in fundamental goods, will be deprived of meaning to the extent that death finds such a person, as it must, with objectives yet to be achieved.

This analysis of action helps us to understand self-determination better. It is not a matter of achieving specific, limited goals, although doing so is in itself proper and necessary, but of participating in fundamental human goods.

Next we shall turn to the question of happiness. Everyone wants to be happy, but at least sometimes most of us are uncertain about what being happy really means. In considering this question we shall stress the notion of fulfillment, meaning by this the most authentic and satisfying happiness of which people are capable. By no means, however, is it immediately apparent what "fulfillment" means either. Thus we shall begin by examining some inadequate notions and then seek, in chapter four, to determine in what fulfillment consists. To anticipate what we shall discover, we shall see that authentic fulfillment corresponds to action at the third level.

Questions for Review and Discussion

1. What is the difference between "person" as we used the word here and "personality" as it is used in psychology or everyday conversation?

2. How does the idea of "person" held by someone who thinks the fundamental problem of life is how to remain or become a person differ from the idea of "person" developed in this chapter?

3. To engage in sexual intercourse as animals do is an action at the first level; to engage in intercourse as a prostitute does is an action at the second level; to engage in intercourse as a deeply loving married couple does, simply to express and celebrate their love of each other, is an action at the third level. Give other examples of actions at different levels, including, if you can, cases in which the outward behavior remains the same.

4. The three levels of action correspond to three senses of freedom distinguished in chapter one. Why aren't there distinct levels of action corresponding to political freedom, ideal freedom, and creative freedom?

5. Do you think that people in our culture, in thinking and speaking about action, usually have in mind second-level or third-level actions? What difference does it make to one's view of life as a whole which of these two levels of action is a person's customary model of action?

6. If third-level action is really determinative of the self, what do the characteristics of this kind of action—for example, the impossibility of calculation—indicate about the sort of reality a person is?

7. Environment is to the organism as situation is to the person. Does an oak tree have the same environment as the cow which is grazing under it?

8. Do you think fictional characters are related to their fictional situations in the same way that real persons are related to their situations?

9. The three levels of action are related to time in different ways. The motto of the first level might be "Live for the present." The motto of the second level might be "Invest in your future." How is the third level of action related to time?

10. Sometimes it is possible to change what one is doing from second-level action to action at the third level simply by a change of intention. But is it always easy to do so? And is it always a good idea?

3: What Fulfillment Isn't

Everyone wants fulfillment, but the obstacles are formidable. It would be naive to suppose that failure to arrive at a correct intellectual understanding of fulfillment is the only one. (After all, one could know perfectly well what fulfillment consists in and yet not be fulfilled.) At the same time, it would be equally naive to suppose that an incorrect understanding cannot contribute to keeping a person from being fulfilled. At the very least, people are more likely to reach a state of fulfillment—whatever it may consist in—if they have a clear and accurate notion of what it means to be fulfilled than if they confuse some other experience or state with this one.

Many people's ideas of fulfillment are dominated by one or the other of two experiences. One is the experience of intense pleasure, typically felt when one reaches the consummation of a first-level action (e.g., that first sip of cold, clear water after a hot and dusty hike). The other is the experience of seeking a future objective, working toward it, and finally attaining it. This is the experience felt when one has the satisfaction of reaching the goal sought in a second-level action. While either of these experiences can be—and often is—mistaken for fulfillment, neither provides a truly good point of departure for understanding it. Each falls short of the fulfillment which we would all like.

1. The Problem with Pleasure

One difficulty in equating intense pleasure with fulfillment is that the experience of pleasure is a value only for a part of the self. In saying this we do not mean to suggest that pleasure is identified with the "lower," "animal" part of human beings and fulfillment with the "higher," "spiritual" part. (We would not accept such a division of the human person into two parts.) The point, instead, is that pleasure—whenever and however experienced—is limited to consciousness and does not take into consideration the living whole of a human being.

To take an extreme example which makes the point quite clear, it is at least conceivable that a person could derive a great deal of pleasure from eating poisoned food—and die as a result of doing so. However pleasurable the individual's state of consciousness might have been while the food was being eaten, one can hardly conclude that the experience was good and fulfilling for this person. This is scarcely what we mean when we speak of fulfillment.

Another problem with pleasure is that we never have it by itself. It always comes riding on the back of some other experience. There is no such thing as an experience of pure pleasure—that is, pleasure and nothing else. And when we reflect upon an enjoyable experience in order, as it were, to isolate the pleasure and enjoy it by itself, the very effort to focus on ourselves and our experience in this way undermines the enjoyable continuation of the action which caused us pleasure in the first place. The harder we try to enjoy ourselves and the more we think about it, the more we defeat ourselves in our effort at enjoyment.

An illustration out of the realm of science fiction dramatizes the problem with pleasure and makes it clear why pleasure does not fulfill a reasonable expectation of what it means to be fulfilled.

Suppose it were possible to keep a human brain alive in a laboratory and feed it a continuous stream of artificial brain waves in order to give it the experience of a constantly pleasurable life. The brain would be in a kind of self-absorbed nirvana, insulated from all pain and at all times enjoying the consciousness of intense pleasure. Would this be worth doing (not from the point of view of scientific experimentation but from the point of bestowing fulfillment upon this particular brain)? Hardly. There would be no point in creating a merely pleasurable state of consciousness, apart from real experience and action in a real world. Even if the thing could be done, it would be meaningless, would make no sense. Whatever else one might say of the pleasure-experiencing brain, no one would call its condition one of human fulfillment.

This points to the fact that states of consciousness, even pleasurable ones, have no meaning and no value in themselves apart from the life which they reflect. A state of consciousness only has meaning in relation to the life of which it is consciousness. If there were really no lived life (as would be the case with the brain in the laboratory), the state of consciousness would be meaningless.

For purposes of ethics, then, it simply confuses matters to talk about pleasure, as a state of consciousness, as if it were a norm for action. Fulfillment, in the sense in which we shall explain it below, provides such a norm. But pleasure is incapable of doing so. Pleasure pertains to action at the first level. And although such action is part of life, the meaning of life cannot be reduced simply to this level.

2. Fulfillment Isn't Looking Ahead

Other thinkers who have sought to understand the meaning of fulfillment have taken as their starting point the experience described earlier: identifying a goal, working to

achieve it, and at last attaining it. This approach locates the
ultimate meaning of life in the outcome of action at the second level. St. Augustine interpreted the Christian promise of
heavenly beatitude in light of the experience of working to
achieve an objective. Today many people who no longer believe in God, heaven, or hell still identify happiness with the
pursuit and attainment of goals and seek happiness in this
experience.

The notion is admittedly attractive, not least because this
kind of action is indeed a necessary and important part of life.
Still, the idea that authentic fulfillment lies in the pursuit and
attainment of goals is not really satisfactory either. As we have
noted earlier, once people achieve one goal, they immediately
begin the pursuit of another. Fulfillment lies always somewhere in the future, and that which lies perpetually in the
future does not meet our expectations of what it should mean
to be fulfilled here and now.

Several considerations make this clear. One problem with
identifying fulfillment with the pursuit of future objectives is
that the objectives *are* future and a person who lives mainly
for the future has to a significant degree robbed the present
of meaning. Living in this way, one in effect makes the present a mere means to an ulterior end, whatever that may be.
In this view of things the present has little or no value in itself;
its value comes instead from what it contributes to or takes
away from the achieving of the objective which we have set for
ourselves.

A life lived in this way is a life half lived. Take the case of a
man whose life was devoted to the goal of climbing Mount
Everest. Let us suppose he cares only about success in reaching his goal, toward which everything else in his life is directed. He spends years in rigorous training: scaling lesser
peaks, developing his skills, organizing his expedition, planning his assault on the final objective. At last the time comes.
He and his party set off up the slopes of Everest. Halfway up,

the mountain climber falls from a ledge and is killed. Everest remains unclimbed.

One's natural reaction to such a story is that the tragic accident robbed the mountain climber's life of meaning. His life was built around the single-minded pursuit of a clearly defined objective: scaling Mount Everest. He never achieved the objective; therefore his failure to achieve it emptied his life of significance. But is this really the case?

Looked at more closely, it appears that the accident cutting short this life spotlighted a glaring fact about it: the life was empty and meaningless all along. How, after all, could reaching the peak of Mount Everest have given retrospective significance to everything that had gone before? For the fact about what has gone before is that it has *gone,* and either there was meaning there all along or there was never any meaning. If the mountain climber's death, short of his goal, makes us conclude that his life was without meaning, this must be because there was never any meaning in it. Even the successful ascent of Everest could not have invested meaning after the fact in the years preceding that event.

As we have said before, we do not intend an indictment of second-level action, by which one identifies specific goals, calculates ways and means of reaching them, and works to achieve them. On the contrary, this way of acting is necessary and appropriate to human life. Failure to perform well at this level can result in a chaotic and ultimately disastrous kind of life reflective of its own particular kind of immoral orientation (a fondness, say, for "spontaneity," meaning a pattern of erratic and self-indulgent behavior, or an ineffectual commitment to "ideals" lacking in the seriousness which causes responsible persons to take practical steps to realize the ideals to which they are committed). Nevertheless, the pursuit of specific goals cannot, by itself, make for a satisfactory and meaningful life; it does not represent an adequate understanding of fulfillment.

The meaning of our lives, if any, exists here and now. Making their meaning hinge on something in the future is tantamount to draining them of meaning. What the man who wished to climb Everest needed was a way of living his life which would have made it rich with meaning whether he succeeded, failed, or died before even setting out on the expedition.

There is another, even more fundamental difficulty in identifying fulfillment with the pursuit of future objectives. It is that, as far as we know, there is no finally satisfactory state. If fulfillment lies somewhere ahead, then—at least in our experience—fulfillment is never reached, for once we achieve one objective, we simply move on to something else. It is a universal human experience that no one goal gives lasting satisfaction. At the instant we possess one thing, we begin to crave something else. If this is fulfillment, then fulfillment must consist in the frustrating experience of never being really satisfied and always seeking something more, something beyond what we already have.

A theologian in the tradition of St. Augustine might reply that this is an accurate enough description of this life, but that this life is not all. The experience of lasting satisfaction, such a theologian would say, is always denied us in this world but is enjoyed after death, in eternal union with God.

Even theologically this is not an acceptable position. For such a theologian also holds that God does nothing useless and depends on nothing to achieve his purposes. But if eternal union with God is all that counts, and if this union is altogether future, then what use does human existence in this world have? Either it has none (in which case God *has* done something useless in causing it to be), or it is a necessary means (in which case God *needs* it for his end), or it has value in itself—which the theologian in the tradition of St. Augustine is not prepared to concede.

Thomas Aquinas, incidentally, took an important step toward resolving the problem by explaining that the value of our present life lies in the fact that in it we share in God's causing of the future, and in doing so we are more like him than if we shared only in his happiness without living through the process of attaining it. One might also argue that it is a mistake to think of *eternal* life as a purely *future* objective, since this is to treat eternity as if it were only another aspect of time.

In any case, to say that our present life derives meaning only from our experience after this life is beside the point as far as ethics is concerned. Ethics deals with this life. It asks whether and how fulfillment can be ours here and now— whether and how actions which we perform at the present time can also make us fulfilled at the present time. As human beings we live from moment to moment. Our lives are made up of these passing moments. To say that fulfillment cannot somehow be found in the unique, passing moments of our lives is to say in effect that human life is meaningless.

The problem of fulfillment, then, comes down to this: How can we be fulfilled continually and how can we be fulfilled now? Fulfillment cannot be mere pleasure, because pleasure is a sometime thing; even as we experience it, it slips away from us—and we have all had the experience of feeling pleasure while knowing in our hearts that we are not really fulfilled. Nor can fulfillment lie in future objectives. If it did, fulfillment would be always deferred, always in the future, and never now. Even when we reach one goal, we immediately begin to crave another. Yet we live our lives now, not in the future, and *now* is where we must find meaning and fulfillment if we are to find them at all.

To put our conclusion in terms of levels of action: neither the pleasure that arises from first-level action nor the pursuit of future objectives and the sense of satisfaction in reaching them which are involved in second-level action can give meaning to human life. We must look toward fulfillment as a fullness of life corresponding to third-level action. Human life derives meaning from participation in fundamental human

goods through third-level action; if such a life is also morally
good, its goodness will arise from doing what has just been
described in a morally good manner. Next we shall begin to
see what this means.

Questions for Review and Discussion

1. Although "pleasure," "joy," "satisfaction," and "happiness" are
closely related in meaning, they have diverse connotations. Explore
the differences, beginning by thinking of cases which exemplify the
special sense of each word.

2. Our argument against identifying pleasure with fulfillment
rests on the premise that pleasure is limited to consciousness and
consciousness is not all there is to a human being. If personality is
equated with consciousness, what is left out?

3. Does someone engaging in an act for sheer pleasure tend to
identify himself with consciousness alone? Compare this with an
act in which one engages with another person or persons and in
which real communication occurs.

4. There is a conflict in our culture at present between middle-
class ideals of achievement and success and the demand for instant
gratification. Discuss this conflict in relation to the ideas about fulfillment developed in this chapter.

5. Marxism condemns religion as the opium of the people—"pie
in the sky when you die." At the same time it argues that the present
generation must be sacrificed for the sake of bringing about a perfect society in the future. Are these positions consistent?

6. Much education is future-directed, organized as a preparation
for later life. Discuss the demand for relevance in education in light
of this chapter's criticism of identifying happiness with future objectives.

7. Why is it that no one goal we reach in life gives lasting satisfaction?

8. If you knew you were going to die—in one year, one month,
one day, or one hour—what difference would that knowledge make
to you? Does the answer tell you anything about the way in which you
find meaning in life at present?

4: Fulfillment Is Being a Complete Person

What is fulfillment? In the last chapter we examined two suggested answers and found them wanting. Fulfillment is not the same thing as fleeting, intense pleasure—an experience limited to consciousness alone. Nor is fulfillment identified with seeking future objectives which, even if achieved, provide only a momentary satisfaction before one sets off restlessly in pursuit of yet other goals.

In seeing what fulfillment is not, however, we have also achieved some insight into what it does mean to be fulfilled. It must be something continuous and here and now, present in each unique moment of our lives. Obviously, though, such a general notion of fulfillment leaves many questions unanswered, including the question of how to *be* fulfilled. We need to look much more closely now at this notion of fulfillment in order to see what it really entails.

1. A Whole Life

Aristotle developed a theory of fulfillment (often translated "happiness") which avoided the mistake of identifying it either with pleasure or with the pursuit and attainment of specific, limited objectives. For Aristotle fulfillment is a whole life in which a human being's peculiar capacity, the ability to reason, is realized both in theoretical knowledge and in rationally guided action.

33

There is much truth in Aristotle's analysis, but it is not the whole truth. He was correct in locating fulfillment in the whole life (rather than in isolated episodes or in future expectations). However, he neglected to consider two other important pieces of the puzzle: the role of self-determination and the fact that other human capacities besides reason make their unique, irreducible contribution to what it means to be fulfilled.

Aristotle looked at human beings from a particular perspective and concluded that their peculiar excellence— that which distinguishes them from every other kind of being in our natural experience—is their reason. But if we consider humans as beings who constitute themselves through their own self-determination—that is, if we consider them as persons—it is clear that other areas of life are equally necessary to the fullness of the person. A person is not a disembodied intellect; a person engages in other kinds of activity besides intellectual activity, and these other spheres of experience also make their special contributions to personhood.

Of course, if we could identify ourselves exclusively with the ideal of rationality, then self-realization and self-fulfillment would lie exclusively in rational activity. The same is true of other purposes and ideals: aesthetic experience, play, even the day-to-day activities necessary for physical survival and well-being. All of these are valid, necessary areas of human activity and experience, and all offer opportunities for self-realization and fulfillment to the extent that they involve and express our freedom of self-determination.

But none of them encompasses the whole of human life and experience. Each is essential, and each, from its own special point of view, is supreme. But no one of them sums up in itself what it means to be a person. To be a person one must respect the unique demands made by each.

We see then that it is not enough to say that fulfillment lies in the use of reason. This is true—fulfillment does lie in the use of reason, but it also lies in the use of our human faculties for physical survival and well-being, for play, and for aesthetic experience. All of these are aspects of a human being.

In creating ourselves as persons through self-determination, we must act in a way that takes all of these spheres of life and experience into account. We must avoid neglecting or violating the values involved in any one of these areas of life, because they are particular aspects of what it means to be a person, and action contrary to any one involves an assault, not on a mere abstraction, but on an aspect of our own personhood. In a true sense this would be a kind of self-mutilation.

By contrast, to be fulfilled will, as Aristotle suggested, mean living a whole life. In order to do this one must take a comprehensive view of what human life is. It is not limited to one area of human capability. Instead it embraces all aspects of the person.

While it is certainly true that no one human being can realize to the full what it means to be a person in all areas of life (and for that matter, no one human being can realize to the full what it means to be a person even in one limited area of life), it is equally true that acting contrary to the values inherent in any of the fundamental spheres of life makes it impossible to lead a whole life and thus renders true fulfillment impossible. In order to be fulfilled, we must, minimally, remain open to all of our possibilities as persons.

2. The Question of Commitment

Mere openness, however, is not enough. Being a person is not something passive; it involves self-determination. Choices are necessary. We must settle for ourselves the issue of how to be the persons that we are.

Self-determination is only possible when calculation is not. Calculation is a necessary part of life, but it does not enter into the action of self-determination (although precise, correct calculation is frequently required to achieve the goals and objectives which make it possible for one's self-determination to express itself in practical, efficacious ways).

A woman wants to buy a reliable used car; therefore she calculates what is necessary to achieve the objective (how to raise the money, how to select a dealer, how to pick out a car, etc.) and performs the required steps in sequence. Her calculations may or may not be correct, and, depending on their correctness, she will or will not achieve her objective: purchasing a reliable automobile at a reasonable price. But the process of calculation is a comparatively simple matter (even though mistakes can be made) because the only question that need be answered about a particular action is whether it contributes to achieving the goal. In other words, the various alternatives can be measured by a common denominator: their effectiveness in reaching the objective. They are accepted or rejected, on the basis of calculation, by how they stack up in relation to the common denominator.

In the case of buying a used car one can approach the task with a literal checklist of criteria which must be met—price, mileage, condition of the engine and the tires, etc.—and which, if met, guarantee successful achievement of the goal. Suppose, though, that the woman buying the car is a mother who needs an auto to carry out a number of her responsibilities in that role. While it is certainly possible to identify a number of specific goals and objectives—such as buying a reliable used car—which both support and express the woman's fundamental commitment, it is clear that the self-determining commitment in question here, that of being a mother, is not subject to the same calculation. Calculation is necessary and important to accomplish many of the specific things which mothers need to accomplish, but on a more profound level, calculation cannot tell a woman whether or how to *be* a mother.

Self-determination is possible and necessary in situations where there is no common reference against which to weigh and measure alternatives. In such situations each alternative is appealing in its own way and in its own frame of reference. One could choose any one of the alternatives and not be mistaken. For in a situation like this, one is not simply making a choice of appropriate means to a limited, well-defined end. One is instead choosing among various purposes which underlie the whole structure of personhood. In choosing this way—choosing one purpose rather than another—we really choose the purposes which will constitute ourselves. We choose the kind of persons we will be.

These acts of self-determination can extend very far; they can in fact control and shape our lives for an indefinite future. An act of this kind is "commitment" in a strict sense.

Such commitment occurs when the act involved has a cumulative aspect, and yet there is no definite end to the accumulation of the particular good. Within such a very large act of commitment there will undoubtedly be a nested sequence of lesser acts which are consistent with and partially fulfill the overarching commitment. Yet no one of these acts by itself totally fulfills the commitment—in no single action does the woman from our earlier example totally realize what it means to be a mother—and in fact all of these acts together do not exhaust the commitment (there always remains some further way of realizing the meaning of motherhood), which is essentially open-ended and always capable of being realized further.

Friendship is a good example of such a commitment. In a friendship there is no point at which one can say, in effect, "So much and no more. I have now fully achieved this friendship and need do nothing more about it." One can of course break off the friendship—but then one is ending the commitment. As long as the commitment—and the friendship—endures, there is no point at which one has finally achieved the friendship and can stop acting in ways which fulfill the commitment.

The life of scholarship provides another example. As long as a person is committed to such a life, he or she goes on accumulating more knowledge, without ever being able to feel that scholarship has finally been achieved and learning can now stop. A person who did decide to stop accumulating knowledge would in effect be deciding to withdraw from the commitment to a life of scholarship.

Marriage provides one of the very best examples of commitment. Jokingly or not, people often say of their marriages, "I didn't realize what I was getting into." Joking aside, they are entirely correct. No one knows what he or she is getting into in making such a commitment, for the simple but profound reason that it is absolutely impossible to foresee (that is, to calculate) all the actions that will be required in living out and living up to the commitment. No one can know what, in practical terms, the reality of marriage will be until he or she has lived through it.

These examples suggest several other important things. First, "commitment" as it is used here is not an ideal; it is very real, even commonplace. For better or worse, everybody makes commitments of one kind or another. Second, commitments, however, are "for better or worse"—that is, the mere fact that one has made a commitment does not mean that it is commendable and good. We shall see more about this later; here it is sufficient to remark that one can, for example, be committed to a life of crime, committed to corrupting and mutually destructive friendships, committed to the pursuit of knowledge for selfish and self-centered reasons, etc. The mere fact that one has made a commitment says nothing about the moral quality of the commitment.

Finally, it would be false to suppose that all commitments are made in a highly self-conscious and explicit way by people reflecting on big issues and options. On the contrary, it is a

common experience that many commitments, even fundamental ones, are backed into by people who do not at any
point in the process advert very clearly to what they are doing.
Very few, for instance, can say precisely when they made the
commitment to marry the person they did marry (this commitment being, clearly, something quite different from proposing or setting the date). Very few know exactly when they
made the commitment to a particular career or vocation.
What appears to happen in many cases is that important
commitments develop incrementally, through a series of relatively minor choices and actions. In particular, this seems to
be a rather common pattern for immoral people. They shape
their lives through many small, bad choices which eventually
box them into a particular commitment—perhaps without
their ever having been fully aware of what was happening—so
that they can no longer see any option except to go on making
more such choices which express and confirm the commitment.

In large, open-ended commitments, in any case, we never
know quite what we are doing when we begin. Only gradually,
through creative effort and experience, do we begin to
understand the meaning of the commitment. And only
gradually do we work out in practice the implications of the
self we have constituted by making the initial commitment.
What we are to be does not exist at the time the commitment
is made; what we are to be is what we *become* through individual actions performed under the umbrella of the fundamental commitment.

There are, in short, two aspects to self-determination
within the framework of a commitment. What we are to be
depends, on the one hand, on our commitment to a purpose
which transcends us and, on the other, to the creative working
out of the implications of that initial commitment in the circumstances of life which we encounter.

One other thing needs to be said here about calculation.

Calculation is definitely possible within a commitment. In fact, it is not merely possible: it is highly advisable to use calculation and technique, as in the case of the woman buying a used car, in order to achieve particular objectives which are consistent with one's commitments. Acting merely on the basis of impulse and emotion, rather than rationality, does not give a more human character to activity, nor is it more likely to be an apt way of realizing one's commitments in practice.

An impulsive gift, for example, is not the best expression of friendship. Rather, a gift that represents the giver's well-considered judgment as to what is most likely to please and benefit the friend is the gift that will best realize friendship in practice. What is important here, however, is that the calculation be directed toward an objective which is itself directed toward participation in and realization of some good. One is not calculating what gift to give simply to keep one's budget in balance; instead the purpose of the calculation is to determine what gift, purchasable within one's budget, will best realize and express the commitment to friendship with one's friend.

3. How Self-determination Works

Actions in and by which we truly constitute ourselves have a number of special characteristics. We have already seen what some of these are, but it will be worthwhile to list them here in order to get a clearer understanding of self-determination. Among the characteristics of such actions, then, are the following:

1. When acting in this way we cannot calculate what behavior will be appropriate for our purpose. As we have seen, calculation comes into play—quite appropriately—in seeking specific, well-defined objectives outside ourselves. But when it

is a question of determining ourselves, technique and calcula-tion will not do the job.

2. We cannot act efficiently in carrying out our commit-ments. There is, for instance, no efficient way to fulfill one's commitment to a friendship or a marriage. Of course one can and should act efficiently in pursuing objectives which are consistent with and help to realize one's basic commitments. But these objectives do not sum up the whole of the commit-ment, which serves as a sort of overarching umbrella under which many specific goals are embraced and many individual actions performed.

3. We cannot force anyone else nor can we ourselves be forced to act in this way. To be sure, it is possible to force somebody else to perform an action, but, by definition, that which one is forced to perform by external pressure is not really an act of self-determination. This is not an argument for never forcing people to do certain things or refrain from doing other things: small children should be required to brush their teeth, emotionally disturbed people should be re-strained from jumping out of windows. The point, however, is that people cannot be forced to determine themselves; they can only determine themselves on the basis of their own choices.

4. In many cases in which we do things we have to do, it is possible to personalize the activity, as it were—to make it an act of self-determination—by consciously locating and choos-ing in it a purpose to which we are or can be committed. One can, for instance, study simply in order to pass a course—period. Or, one can study in order to pass a course in order to get a degree which will make it possible to pursue a profession to which one is truly committed. Or, one can study just for the sake of increasing one's knowledge (with passing the course a kind of desirable by-product). In the latter two cases the act of studying has become more personally meaningful, because it

relates to a commitment which expresses one's self-determination. We can frequently make the necessary events and activities of our lives more meaningful in this way. That is not to say one should not try to change unsatisfactory conditions in one's life and society that can and should be changed. It is only to point out a way of deriving the most meaning from parts of life that cannot or should not be changed.

5. Observation of outward behavior by itself cannot decisively establish whether or not a person is acting through commitment. To go back to our example, the student studying simply to pass a course will very likely *look* the same and perform the same external actions as the student studying out of love of learning for its own sake. The difference is not in their outward behavior but in their intentions.

These five characteristics have one thing in common: all illustrate the fact that self-determining action for a purpose intrinsic to the action is quite different from action which is determined by its orientation to an extrinsic goal. However much alike such actions may look from the outside, they are in fact radically different on the inside.

In determining ourselves through our commitments we shape our lives. We establish our way of looking at things. We determine the meaning of the experiences we will have. Thus, as we have seen earlier, we really create situations in a moral sense, because we give the events of our lives and the facts of the world the unique meaning which they have *for us*. This is in sharp contradiction to the argument of so-called situation ethics, which implies that the meaning of a situation is something given, over which we have no control and which we can only passively accept.

How then are we complete persons? This will be the case if our commitments meet certain criteria (which we shall discuss later), if they all fit together to form a harmonious whole, and if we live our lives out in accord with such a harmonious set of commitments. Then we shall be complete persons. And this is what fulfillment is.

It is clear, though, that as persons living in social relationships with other persons, we do not find completion in isolation from others. On the contrary, other people play a crucial role in our being the persons we are. In the next chapter we shall look at some of the implications of this fact.

Questions for Review and Discussion

1. Explain how Aristotle's notion of fulfillment resembles but is also significantly different from the one presented here.

2. What are some possible reasons why Aristotle overlooked the capacity of self-determination as central to the human person?

3. What implications might the differences between Aristotle's position and the authors' have as far as issues involving "mere life" are concerned—for instance, the question of capital punishment or the question of euthanasia for the senile or insane?

4. "Choice" has two senses, corresponding to the second and third levels of action. Distinguish these two senses from each other.

5. Make a diagram representing the relationship between the subordinate ends, intermediate ends, and a final goal in second-level action. Make a different diagram expressing the relationship between subordinate acts and the overarching commitment in third-level action.

6. To what extent can expressions like "subjective" and "objective," "fixed" and "indeterminate," apply to diverse aspects of a commitment?

7. Why (in terms of the analysis of commitment in this chapter) do newly married couples often begin to experience difficulties as soon as the honeymoon ends?

8. Some people talk about an "art of living" as if there were an applied science (such as psychology) which could give us directions for living a good life. If the position developed in this chapter is correct, can there be an "art of living" in this sense? Leaving aside what is said in this chapter, what arguments can you think of for or against the possibility of devising an art of living?

9. We cannot force anyone else to make a commitment, nor can we ourselves be forced to do so. How, then, can people have any effect at all on one another's commitments?

10. Sociologists dealing with topics involving religion often experience serious difficulty in finding objective criteria by which to measure how "religious" different people are. Why do you think this is so?

11. It may be impossible to tell apart the outward behavior of a person acting for an intrinsic goal and that of another person committed to doing what he is doing for its own sake. But if you know two people well, it is likely that you will see certain signs of their true attitude. Apart from what they say if asked, what might such signs include?

5: Persons Complete
One Another

"No man is an island," wrote John Donne. "Hell is other people," according to a character in a play by Jean-Paul Sartre. For better or worse (sometimes better, sometimes worse) each of us is linked to many other people by an intricate network of social relationships. Sociologists, political scientists, and other specialists make this evident fact of human life an object of constant study and analysis. For the student of ethics, too, it raises great and lasting issues. What sorts of relationships are possible between individual persons? And what moral significance do these relationships have?

For some philosophers a human being is primarily a self-seeking individual. In this view society is an artificial creation: a framework for the operation of individual selfishness, an arena within which the powerful can exploit the weak or the many can control the few. Others take a radically different point of view and hold that the community is the central reality. For them individual personality is only a sort of abstraction. Here we shall take the position that neither of these extremes is correct and the truth about human relationships is situated in a middle ground.

1. Others As Objects

Not all human relationships are the same. The relationship between two strangers sitting side by side on a bus is not the

same as the relationship between a husband and wife. Nor is
the relationship between either of these pairs the same as that
between a bank teller and a holdup man who has just deliv-
ered the ultimatum: "Hand over the money, or else!" But it is
not saying a great deal to state merely that these relationships
are not the same. We must look more closely in order to see
where the basic differences lie.

In many human relationships people treat each other as
objects. We have all been conditioned to regard treating others as objects as a bad thing, and in fact the consequences can
be grim, being reflected in such things as wartime body
counts and the gas chambers in the Nazi concentration camps.

Yet for all that, this others-as-objects approach is not necessarily immoral. Sometimes it is entirely appropriate. An engineer seeking to determine the capacity of an elevator sets
the limit at a certain number of passengers, based not on their
peculiarly individual characteristics but simply on the average
weight of the bodies to be carried. It would not help the
engineer—indeed, it might make his task impossible—if he
had to take into consideration the personalities of the unique
individuals who would actually ride in the elevator.

There are also other human relationships, somewhat more
complex and intimate, which involve a degree of recognition
of human potentiality but still do not constitute genuine
community. In ordinary circumstances two strangers sharing
a bus seat do not, and need not, enter into a relationship of
community; but each does need to recognize the other's
human needs and rights, at least to the extent of allowing the
other enough room to sit comfortably.

Many formal contractual relationships are basically of the
same kind. The parties to the contract do not need to share
common interests, commitments, and points of view beyond
the very limited area required to make the arrangement
work. And the arrangement works when the objectives which
drew the parties together in the first place are achieved.

However, such arrangements do not always work. One bus rider can take up more than his or her fair share of the seat. One party to a contract can manipulate the terms of the agreement, or violate them, in such a way as to injure the other party or parties. In such cases, where the advantage of the relationship is tipped too far in one direction, the others-as-objects approach becomes exploitative and unjust.

No doubt it is already clear from this analysis that this sort of relationship, in which other persons are viewed and treated as objects, is appropriate to action at the second level: action, that is, which is directed to achieving some specific, extrinsic goal. It should also be apparent that this way of dealing with others, although it can be abused, is a necessary, important, and entirely proper part of human life in society. Some human relationships, however, are based not on the seeking of particular limited objectives but on mutual commitment to the same value or values. The relationship in such a case is what we call "community."

2. Others As Community

In a community, whether very large or very small, a certain number of individuals continue to perform their individual, separate, third-level actions: basic, self-determining acts of commitment and also the acts by which they express and realize their commitment in concrete situations. In a real sense, however, there is more here than just the sum total of all the actions of the individual community members. When two or more people unite for the joint realization of a basic good to which they are committed, a community itself is constituted by the common social act—an act which is more than the individual actions of the community members.

The members of a genuine community truly overcome their individual isolation, since, understanding and endorsing one another's commitment, they become common agents of a single action. Of course, each community member may well act differently, doing what is appropriate to his or her own special role in the community; but at the same time the unity of meaning, the shared commitment, underlying these different actions flows into a single action, in whose performance the community members become one.

We do not wish to romanticize community, as the word is used here. There is a popular sense of the word which takes it for granted that "community" means commitment only to good purposes, besides involving only mutually loving relationships among the community members. This may be a true picture, more or less, of some communities, but it is not necessarily true of all. A band of terrorists or a fanatical religious cult is also an example of community, as we are using the word. Good community implies proper commitment to good purposes expressed in suitable behavior; a bad community is one in which either the purposes or the behavior or both are morally wrong.

It is not necessary for each member of the community to engage in all of the community's behavior. What is necessary is that the behavior of each member be appropriate to his or her role in the community, that it embody a working-out of the commitment shared with all the other members of the community.

Not all members of a basketball team, for instance, do the same thing. The center has one job to do, the forwards and guards other jobs. However, by playing a special role on the team each makes a particular contribution to the realization of the commitment which brought the team together in the first place and continues to hold it together.

A basketball team, however, is a very simple example of community. Many communities are far larger and more complex. A nation is also a community, and in the United States the Preamble to the Constitution is a verbal enactment of the common action constituting the community. It is an attempt to express in words the values and the commitment to realize those values shared by the members of this national community.

The example of the nation as a form of community underlines the complexity of this whole question. So, for instance, the individuals who originally participated in the formation of the particular community called the "United States" died long ago; yet the same social act continues to exist today with new individuals participating in it.

It is also clear that much more is needed for true community than simply a shared commitment to a value or a set of values. As we have seen, it is also necessary that the individual community members act, in ways appropriate to their positions in the community, in order to realize the values to which they are committed.

Furthermore, in a very large community, such as a nation, there is need for an extremely complicated intermediate structure—laws, institutions—between the joint social act constituting the community and the multitude of individual acts performed by the community members as they work to realize their shared commitment. The alternative to such a rational, intermediate structure is, in large communities, chaos.

Another evident fact about large communities such as nations is that it is unrealistic to think of them in terms of third-level action alone. To be sure, third-level action is central to community: there must be a basic commitment to some fundamental human value or values, coupled with a determination to realize the value or values through concrete action in concrete circumstances. But realizing values in practice necessarily calls for the calculated pursuit of goals which express and are instrumental to this realizing of values: it calls, in

other words, for second-level action, directed, at least immediately, not to participation in some basic human good but
to the achieving of limited, specific objectives.

This is not a criticism of communities. Individuals often
do, and must, act for limited goals; and so do, and must,
communities if they are to survive—if, indeed, they are to
realize their basic commitments. The important thing, for
both individuals and communities, is that the specific objectives and the means chosen to achieve them be shaped by, or
at least not be in contradiction to, the basic values to which the
individual or community is committed. The reason why
second-level action may tend to lessen the communal character of communities is that in practice it is often directed to
individual objectives that violate the common purposes of the
community as such: as when a basketball team spends so
much time seeking publicity that it no longer functions well
on the court or a religious group devotes itself so heavily to
business ventures and fund-raising that its religious purposes
are lost sight of.

3. Individual, Society, and Societies

Most people act most of the time as officials. This may
sound like a surprising statement, but it is evidently true,
provided one understands "official" to mean anyone acting in
his or her capacity as a member of a community. To put the
matter another way, most of what we all do is done as an
expression of our roles in one community or another. All of
us belong to many different communities, and we are constantly acting as members of them.

Consider some communities to which a typical person may
belong: the community called "marriage," the community
called "the family," the community called "the company," the
community called "the church," the community called "the

nation," the community called "the university," communities
called "the team," "the club," "the gang," "the neighborhood,"
"my best friendship," and so on. One could continue indefi-
nitely. Any individual, upon reflection, can put together an
extremely long list of communities to which he or she belongs
and will probably overlook some in the process.

The point is that each of us has not just a few social roles
but many different ones, depending on which particular society or societies are in question at any given time. And in the
normal course of events almost everything we do is done by
virtue of membership in one or another of these societies. It is
a tendency of human action to be communal and social in
nature.

We belong to some societies because we have chosen to
belong. We belong to others without really having made an
explicit choice. Most people, for example, become citizens of a
particular nation, and therefore members of that particular
national community, by an accident of birth, not as a result of
their own deliberate choice.

This is a practical convenience in many ways, but it can also
present grave difficulties for an individual. By reason of
membership in a particular community one can become involved in a communal act without any decision on one's part,
and perhaps without even knowing of it (as happens, for instance, in the case of infants and children who are involved in
the actions of the various communities into which they have
been born). Difficulties arise when a community to which one
belongs undertakes a communal action with which one cannot
conscientiously agree. If, for instance, one's country becomes
involved in a war which one regards as unjust, very hard
choices, imposed by membership in that national community,
must be faced.

An individual's role in society consists of the various things
that he or she may do—and some of which he or she is obliged
to do—in virtue of participation in the society. Roles are not

catalogues of things which individuals actually do; rather they can be thought of as lists of things persons can do and in some cases should do because of the positions they occupy in the community.

A society or community requires for its continued existence that its individual members fulfill the requirements of their various roles. In a sense, therefore, each member of the society is dependent on every other member.

It is true of course that an individual can fail to meet some of the requirements of his or her role without destroying the social act and, thereby, the society. A marriage can continue to exist even if one or both partners are something less than punctilious in carrying out their respective marital roles. A nation can continue to exist even if some citizens neglect some or all duties of citizenship. At the same time, however, there is in every society a certain minimal level of role fulfillment, varying with the society, which is essential if the community is going to continue to be. If a significant number of the members of a society (the significant number will be different for different societies) fall below this level, the community will simply disintegrate.

We have already seen that everyone belongs to many different societies and, as a result, has a number of different social roles. This can very well raise problems for an individual as far as self-determination is involved. The first and fundamental necessity is of course to opt for membership in morally good communities—those committed to good purposes pursued in good ways—and avoid membership in vicious and corrupt ones. But beyond that, people face the significant challenge of selecting their communities in a way that makes their lives unified wholes.

If membership in one society requires a commitment and forms of behavior which are in conflict with the commitment and behavior demanded by membership in another society, something has to give. Normally a man cannot be a functioning member of both the community called "marriage" and a community of monks; it is difficult to be a participating member of a pacifist organization while also being a participating member of the armed forces.

These are extreme examples, but more subtle and complicated ones often arise. Indeed, in times like ours, when people ordinarily enjoy many different opportunities and options—to belong or not to belong to many different societies—the problem of harmonizing social roles and avoiding conflicts of duty can be very serious.

4. Authority

This analysis of societies should help to shed some light on what is today a rather sensitive issue: the role of authority.

In second-level relationships (situations involving specific means to well-defined objectives) "authority" is virtually synonymous with "power." Authority is involved in such relationships when one person sets down requirements and obliges another person or persons to fulfill them. The person exercising authority here is simply exercising managerial power. And although "authority" and "power" have rather a bad name today, it is important to bear in mind that this state of affairs is necessary and entirely correct in many circumstances.

The situation is, however, quite different in cases of true community, where a third-level social act (a commitment to a shared value or values and to actions expressive of this value system) is involved. Here the role of authority is to articulate the common, overall social act and to plan the organization of behavior by members of the community so as to realize their common purposes. Authority in such a situation, too, is not an inherently bad thing; on the contrary, it is simply necessary. Furthermore, it can be a form of service to the community rather than a way of exercising power over the community.

In real life, though, authority does become a problem, in
part at least because of the mixed nature of many societies.
They are neither wholly third level nor wholly second level
but something of both. As a result, the role of authority is
similarly mixed: a combination of service and power. This,
too, is neither good nor bad—it is just a fact of life. But it does
open the door to abuses.

One of these, on the side of authority, is to make abusive,
exploitative use of power and sometimes, in doing so, to pretend that it is service. This is the accepted style of dictators
and tyrants, both large and small, who present themselves as
"protectors of the common good" and "servants of the
people" while in fact pursuing their own interests and exploit-
ing the people whom they profess to serve.

The problem, however, does not lie exclusively on the side
of authority. The other members of the community also can
abuse the relationship. This comes about in the case of individuals or groups which seek to enjoy a free ride: taking advantage of the benefits which come from belonging to the
community while avoiding making the appropriate contribution to the community required by their social role. It is a
temptation, one frequently succumbed to, for people in this
position to attack authority as "exploitative." Doing so, after
all, gives these free-loaders a measure of ostensible justification for failing to carry their fair share of the burden of
making the community work.

5. Community and Human Purposes

No one person can actively pursue, much less realize, all
the purposes for which human beings are capable of striving.
Life is short, the abilities of any one person are limited, and in
committing oneself to seek to realize some purposes, one inevitably gives up the possibility of striving actively for others.

In a real sense, however, community compensates for our individual limitations by making possible the realization, or at least an attempt at the realization, of human purposes which any one of us singly is incapable of realizing. United in community, persons are able to respond to the demands for active service made by all the goods.

Thus community—common commitment—need not take the form of people actively working together on behalf of the same purposes. More fundamentally, community, understood and realized in a morally right way, means that each member of the community recognizes and respects the fundamental human purposes to which other members of the community are dedicated. To be sure, real-life communities, even the best, commonly contain at least some admixture of selfishness and exploitation; and communities at their worst can be debased caricatures of communities at their best: settings in which people seek vicious ends in vicious ways. Still, the ideal of community remains and, sometimes at least, exists in real life. In such a community, recognition and respect for the goods to which other members are committed express themselves in appreciation of the particular interests and ways of life of others, and in satisfaction at their accomplishments. At the heart of community lies the sense that it is more important that the good be realized than that I, as an individual, realize it for myself.

Some people deny that genuine love of others is possible. It would *not* be possible if loving others meant that we had to seek an alien good—a good which was foreign to us and in which we felt we had no part. It is possible for us to love one another, however, if we are committed to seeking together a good or goods which we feel to be our own and yet recognize as "bigger than all of us."

Others, viewing the individual as all but obliterated in society, deny the significance of individuals and their unique responsibility. But genuine community does not come about by denying our individuality, our otherness, in a blind effort to submerge ourselves in an anthill society. Community is based instead on a shared commitment in which each individual shoulders his or her special share of the responsibility for realizing the values which originally drew separate persons into the relationship called "community."

Up to this point we have learned something about the meaning of freedom, about the various kinds or levels of action, and in particular about the kind of action which is self-determination. We have considered fulfillment, which is closely tied to freedom of self-determination. And we have looked at the crucial role of social relationships. All this, however, has only laid the groundwork for determining what makes action morally good or bad. It is time now to begin to consider this central question. Our first step will be to examine and criticize views that would make it impossible to say for sure what is right and what is wrong.

Questions for Review and Discussion

1. One theory of society is the organic view, which sees the individual as hardly more than an abstraction from the social whole. This is sometimes called "the anthill society." Do you know of any specific theories of this sort, or any historical attempts to bring into reality societies which conform to such a model?

2. Large corporations (and other organizations) spend a great deal of money on personnel offices and public relations staffs to try to personalize their relationships with employees and customers. In what circumstances and to what extent can such efforts be genuine?

3. In a true community what unites the members into a single whole? What distinguishes them so that they do not get lost in that whole?

4. Some people fear loving and being loved because they are afraid of losing their identity in too close a relationship. Do you think such a fear can be well grounded? If so, how can the problem be overcome?

5. Analyze the Preamble to the U.S. Constitution as an example of a community-forming act. Compare this with mutually exchanged wedding vows as another example of a community-forming act.

6. Can the same society simultaneously involve aspects of genuine community, of contractual relation, and of exploitation? Why would it be important to take account of these various forms of relationship in order to understand the behavior of people in a society?

7. Compare the problem of integrating social roles faced by a person in contemporary society with the problem faced by a member of a primitive tribe.

8. Some ethical theories give a very special place to the political community, going so far as to hold that ordinary ethics does not apply to it. According to the theory presented here, the political community is only one among others and not exempt from the claims of ordinary ethics. Why is this so?

9. Find and discuss concrete examples to illustrate the different meanings of authority and the ambivalence present in relationships which involve authority.

10. Community is impossible among people who do not think that there is anything bigger than both (or all) of us. Does this "something bigger" necessarily imply that there is some superhuman reality, such as God?

6: We Don't Always Know What Is Good for Us

We are free to choose what we will do. But we are not free to make whatever we choose right.

We must follow our best judgment concerning what we ought to do. But our best judgment can be mistaken.

For many people these four propositions are self-evident and unassailable. For many others they are neither—indeed, they are flatly untrue. These propositions contradict various forms of relativism and subjectivism which are prevalent today and which, for the beginner at least, constitute a major obstacle to serious reflection regarding ethical issues.

What is meant here by "relativism" and "subjectivism"? The words do not commonly come up in conversation, but the attitudes they stand for are commonplace. How often, for example, when it is a question of whether a particular action is right or wrong, does one hear it said "It all depends on what the society you live in regards as good" or "It all depends on the kind of life you want to live"? Shorthand expressions like these sum up a whole approach (at least, a conscious approach) to ethical problems: "It all depends. . . ."

Of course, in a certain sense it all *does* depend. Decisions about the right and wrong of actions depend on many different factors, including those so strongly emphasized by cultural relativism and individualistic subjectivism. As with many other approaches to ethical questions, relativism and subjectivism are not totally devoid of truth. The trouble is that they have fastened upon particular truths and, in doing so, have excluded other aspects of reality which must be taken into consideration in developing a well-rounded ethics which respects the facts of experience. They are not totally divorced from reality; rather they are distortions—distortions because they single out certain aspects of reality and ignore others.

Relativism and subjectivism make ethics (that is, the serious and sustained examination of one's life and society from the viewpoint of what actions should and should not be performed) a virtual impossibility. It is true that they can properly be described as ethical theories. But they are ethical theories which cut short the ethical enterprise. They deny in principle that moral judgments can be simply true or false.

If it were the case that no moral judgment is simply true or false, the effort to examine one's life or one's society by methods of rational criticism would be ultimately pointless. For the conclusion of any such examination would always be "It all depends on the kind of life you want to live" or "It all depends on what the society you live in regards as good." This marks a dead end to any reasoned effort to decide what actions are right and what actions are wrong, and why.

It should be apparent by now that the position we are taking is reflected in the series of propositions at the start of this chapter. "We are free to choose what we will do. But we are not free to make whatever we choose right. We must follow our best judgment concerning what we ought to do. But our best judgment can be mistaken." It is not enough, however, simply to assert these things. In order to hold and develop these positions, it is necessary first to get over the hurdle posed by relativism and subjectivism. This is what we shall now undertake to do.

1. Cultural Relativism

Cultural relativism is an offspring of anthropology, the study of the customs and beliefs of cultures. Although cultural relativism is rejected by many contemporary anthropologists, it continues to have an impact on popular attitudes.

At one time or another everyone has encountered cultural relativism. The conversation turns at a party to some exotic practice—human sacrifice perhaps—and invariably the cultural relativist in the crowd will say something like, "Well, if those people really believed (or believe) that it was the right thing to do, I suppose it was right *for them*." This expresses the view that norms of right and wrong action are totally derived from the society in which one lives; there is no other criterion of right and wrong than what one's own society happens to believe on the matter, since in the last analysis all such norms are determined by social conditioning and by the circumstances and needs of particular cultures.

Upon reflection most people instinctively draw back from wholehearted acceptance of cultural relativism; they do not really care to be in the position of saying that such things as human sacrifice or cannibalism or ritual prostitution are good and proper if society happens to regard them as such. There are, however, better reasons for rejecting cultural relativism than the instinctive repugnance people feel for the conclusions to which it logically leads (even though that instinctive repugnance is itself not without significance in the matter).

For one thing, as we have noted, cultural relativism is now losing support even in the professional anthropological circles where it once prevailed. It is perfectly true that there are striking differences between the ethical values of particular cultures. But these differences are to a great extent explicable in view of differences in physical conditions, beliefs, knowledge and ignorance, levels of scientific and technical progress, and other accidents of history prevailing at different times in different societies. Given such factual differences, even a single set of universally valid norms can be expected to yield strikingly different concrete judgments. One need not, in other words, postulate cultural relativism as an ethical theory in order to account for the fact of ethical diversity among various cultures.

More fundamentally, contemporary anthropology has pierced beyond the surface of the differences which distinguish one culture from another and succeeded in identifying the basic points of convergence in which superficially very different cultures are in fact very much alike. Cultures have come to be seen as ways in which human beings seek to satisfy common, underlying human needs. These needs correspond, as far as the testimony of contemporary anthropology can tell us, to certain basic, universal human goods.

Consider an example. Life is a basic good: a value respected, so far as the evidence shows, at all times in all cultures. This is not to say that all cultures have expressed their sensitivity to and respect for life in the same way. On the contrary, very primitive tribal cultures limit their respect for life to members of the tribe, the group, those who are identified—by whatever criteria—as belonging to "us."

In other cultures respect for the value of life is extended to embrace others who are not identifiably part of the small ingroup, until, ideally, respect for human life is extended to all those who possess life (a point at which, possibly, no culture in history has yet truly arrived, and which is certainly beyond the moral grasp of contemporary culture). In spite of the extreme diversity, however, centering basically on the question of who are and are not members of the group whose lives deserve respect, the important fact is that every culture in some way manifests awareness of and respect for the value of life.

The same is true of many other basic human goods: the

begetting and raising of children, which has always been recognized as a central value by every culture; intellectual
knowledge; play or recreation; and so on. Clearly there has
been enormous variety in the ways by which particular
societies have expressed their recognition of these values, and
clearly, too, there is a true relativity of duties, since these vary
according to the institutions and practices of particular
societies and the various roles of individuals in them (property rights, for example, vary according to the economic
structure of the society). But beyond the differences, running
as permanent threads through all cultures has been the recognition that such values are important and indeed fundamental to human life. Cultural relativism represents too su-
perficial an analysis: one which, in emphasizing the differences among cultures, fails to take into account the basic
sameness below the surface.

Apart from these considerations, cultural relativism has
become increasingly irrelevant in our times for the simple
reason that distinct cultures, as historically understood and
studied by anthropology, are disappearing. Today perhaps
no truly isolated group is left in the world—no group unaf-
fected by the beliefs and attitudes of other groups—and if
there should be such, it seems certain to vanish in the near
future under the impact of communications technology.

Our world indeed appears to be moving toward the day,
perhaps not too far off, when it will no longer be possible to
speak of "cultures" but only of a single "world culture" in
which local variations of belief and custom are of rather
minor significance. As this state of affairs emerges, it becomes
increasingly artificial to attempt to apply the concept of cultural relativism to the realities of life.

Finally, as a practical matter, if one were to be consistent in
espousing cultural relativism, one would logically have to
apply this theory to one's own culture; and doing so would
make it impossible to criticize values of the society in which

one lives. For if ethical values are endowed with validity simply by the fact that a culture accepts them, there is no ground
on which a person can reasonably criticize the ethical status
quo of any existing society, even if that status quo involves the
policy of *apartheid* or the functioning of the Gulag Ar-
chipelago.

The effect of this is to make efforts to achieve reasoned
social change impossible. Instead, social change comes to depend on the ability of individuals and groups to impose their
will, their vision of how things ought to be, on other individuals and groups in society—a power struggle rather than a
debate.

2. Individualistic Subjectivism

Even more prevalent, perhaps, than cultural relativism is
the attitude known as individualistic subjectivism. It is based
on the belief that individuals spin their own moral norms out
of their own interiors and that, ultimately, the only criterion
for judging behavior, one's own or someone else's, is consistency. That is, the only ethical judgment possible is that persons either are or are not living according to the standards
they have set for themselves: "It all depends on the kind of
life you want to live."

If this position is correct, it makes no sense to argue either
for or against any moral proposition about which different
people hold different views. There is no standard according
to which one can maintain that, say, the dropping of the
atomic bomb on the civilian population of Hiroshima was
wrong—or, for that matter, that it was right. Assuming that
the people who made and executed the decision were doing
what they thought they should do, one can only agree that
undoubtedly what they did was the right thing for them to do.

Yet people evidently do attempt to argue for and against

such moral propositions, almost as if they intuitively recognize that there are moral norms which transcend the limits of individual preference and consistency and apply to many (perhaps all) people. In practice, no one concedes that differences about fundamental moral issues are on the same level as differences of taste concerning such things as music and movies.

If subjectivism were correct, however, it would mean that in the end no one could ever do anything really wrong, except through lack of ingenuity. We are after all free to choose what we will do, and if that freedom can make what we choose right, who would ever choose to do anything while choosing at the same time to make it wrong?

It might be objected that in this view of things "inconsistency" (not living up to one's subjective standards of behavior) is "immorality," and that it is quite possible for a person to be inconsistent, and therefore immoral, as a result of confusion or inconstancy. But one can easily enough be consistent without being constant, provided one is ingenious enough to incorporate so many qualifications and limitations into moral decisions that no particular decision is ever really binding, as a matter of consistency, in the future. All that "consistency" in this sense requires is enough sophistication to arrange things so that inconsistency becomes a practical impossibility.

In any case, a closer look at subjectivism discloses that the whole theory is built on ambiguity and confusion in the use of language. Subjectivism comes down to this: Whatever a person decides is right, is right for him or her. But the word "decide" is being used here to refer to two very different things: judgment and choice. We decide (judge) what is right, and we also decide (choose) what we will do. But the two kinds of deciding are not the same, and subjectivism goes wrong in ignoring the fact.

It is likewise necessary to make a distinction between the

rightness or wrongness of what we do and our individual guilt or innocence in choosing to do it. It is possible to commit atrocities with a good heart, just as it is possible to do good deeds with evil intentions. In the first case the goodness of the intention has no effect on the badness of the deed; just as in the second the goodness of the deed has no effect on the badness of the intention. The intention and the action are and remain distinct, and each must be considered in making judgments about the morality of one's own or other people's action.

If, finally, subjectivism were correct, we could not help knowing what is morally right for us to do. However, that which is morally right for us, whatever it may be, must surely be that which is, in the moral sphere, most profoundly good for us as persons. Yet our common experience tells us that we do not always know what is really good for us in other areas of life: in matters affecting our health, for example, or our vocational choice. And if it is frequently so difficult for us to know what is best for us in other areas of life, why assume that it should be so simple in the moral sphere—so simple, indeed, that whatever we choose is automatically the best thing for us? None of our beliefs and attitudes in other areas of life are beyond rational examination and criticism. Why suppose that it is different in the moral domain?

Sometimes a kind of transference occurs. Ethical subjectivism is imputed to authority—not as an aberration (which can indeed be the case) but as something inherent both to authority and to the making of ethical decisions. This view is expressed in such a challenge as "Who makes the rules—and why should I be bound by someone else's rules?" Essentially, however, ethics is concerned with neither making nor enforcing rules. It is concerned with finding standards—moral truths—which no one makes. And if, as we have argued here, it is not true to say that we make whatever we choose right by the fact of choosing, then clearly we stand in need of standards to apply in making our choices: standards by which we can determine whether the things we choose are right and also whether our reasons for choosing them are right. In the chapters that follow we shall try to show what those standards are.

Questions for Review and Discussion

1. Why are relativism and subjectivism in principle incompatible with the position that ethical judgments can be simply true or false?

2. Are white South Africans members of a different culture from that of black South Africans; from that of white Americans; from that of black Americans?

3. The truth underlying cultural relativism is that, as a matter of fact, there are wide differences between the ethical values of particular cultures. Why doesn't this settle the ethical issue in favor of relativism?

4. Some cultural relativists used to criticize members of Western societies for their intolerance of the primitive ways of less civilized groups. Do you see any incompatibility between offering such criticism and holding the theory of cultural relativism?

5. Why is an affirmation of freedom of self-determination compatible with the denial of subjectivism?

6. Distinguish between subjectivism and the position which says that each person is obliged to do what he or she sincerely believes to be right (the obligation to follow one's conscience).

7. If subjectivism were correct, would it make sense to say of an individual that "He is guiltless when he does what he sincerely believes is right, even though he happens through no fault of his own to be mistaken in this belief"?

8. As a matter of fact, more people are likely to express a subjectivist attitude on questions of sexual morality than on questions of social justice, such as racial discrimination. Again, some people who were absolutely certain that the Vietnam war was immoral hold a subjectivist position on such issues as the morality of the use of drugs. Do such differences necessarily mark inconsistencies? How can such differences be explained?

9. Rejecting relativism and subjectivism doesn't mean that one must hold that all people in all places at all times have exactly the same moral obligations. Can you think of reasons why—even though moral judgments are objectively true or false—different people should have different moral obligations?

7: Purposes—Ulterior and Otherwise

If subjectivism and cultural relativism are not adequate guides in the difficult task of judging human action—our own and others'—we must look elsewhere for such assistance. The search is not easy. But an examination of the purposes for which people act provides an important step in the right direction.

At the outset a note about terminology. The purposes we shall be discussing can just as well be called "goods." In this context, however, the use of the word "good" does not mean that we have reached the stage of being able to discriminate between what is *morally* good and bad. At this point we are using the word "good" simply to refer to a possible purpose of third-level action, whether it be morally good or bad.

Also, the purposes or goods we shall consider here are very broad in scope—so broad, in fact, that it is difficult to find a single label which adequately describes any one category. The reader should understand that the labels we use are attempts at identification, not precise definition.

1. Purposes

Everyone has heard the expression "ulterior motive." When we say that a person has an ulterior motive, we mean

68

that the purpose for which he or she is acting is being sought not for its own sake but for the sake of something else, as a means to an end. There is nothing wrong or unusual about this. People commonly act in this way, and there is no reason to criticize an office worker, say, who does her job not exclusively or even mainly for its own sake but in order to earn what she needs to support herself and her family.

At the same time there are purposes which, although they can be and frequently are sought as means to ends, can also be sought simply for their own sakes, without reference to anything else. Unless he has extraordinary presence of mind, a drowning man struggling to keep his head above water is simply striving to stay alive; he is *not* trying to save himself because of some further purpose to which he wishes to dedicate his life. Unless she is unusually calculating, a child absorbed in piecing together a jigsaw puzzle is working the puzzle simply for its own sake, not in order to please her parents or improve her mind. Unless they are unusually insensitive, people listening to a beautiful or stirring piece of music are enjoying the music for its own sake, not because they have bought concert tickets and want to show their neighbors how cultured they are.

These simple examples illustrate the fact that there are purposes or goods for which one can act for their own sake, without reference to any other purpose. They also illustrate the fact that the same purposes can be and sometimes are sought as means to ends beyond themselves. The emphasis here, however, is on the first characteristic of these goods: one can act for their sake and their sake alone. It is in such purposes that one can participate by third-level action. On closer examination it appears that they fall into several categories.

One group of purposes can be lumped together under the heading "life." This category clearly includes the preservation of life: so-called "matters of life or death." But it also includes various aspects of life, such as health, safety, and the avoidance or removal of pain. Also encompassed here is procreation, the begetting of new life and the nurturing of children; for a couple can desire to have a child for no other reason than that they want to have a child.

A second group of purposes can be labeled "play." This category includes games and sports, all the things one normally thinks of as play, but it also includes a great deal else. It is possible for a person to engage in extremely taxing and strenuous activity, physical or mental, and still be playing, even though a casual observer might be disposed to call the activity work. People are in play situations whenever they engage in performances simply because they enjoy the performances themselves. If it is done just because the individual doing it likes it, the next person who swims the English Channel or goes over Niagara Falls in a barrel will be playing.

A third group of purposes which can be sought for their own sake lies in the area of "aesthetic experience." This includes not only such things as enjoying works of art like symphonies and paintings but other, superficially very different experiences. The pleasure one takes from contemplating a beautiful scene in nature can be an aesthetic experience. So can the pleasure one takes from watching a football game on television. Obviously there are specific differences between a football game and a ballet, yet watching either can involve a genuine aesthetic experience. An aesthetic experience is one which a person seeks because the experience itself is valued, not because it leads to anything beyond itself; unlike play, however, aesthetic experience involves, not a performance of one's own, but rather the internal experiencing of something which comes to one from outside.

Still another group of purposes can be labeled "speculative knowledge." As might be expected, speculative knowledge is knowledge which is sought for its own sake, not for its usefulness as a means to some other end. It is, quite simply, knowl-

edge sought to satisfy curiosity. Because "speculative knowledge" sounds rather formidable, one might tend to identify it
solely with the activity of such apparently detached thinkers
as philosophers and physicists. But the quest for speculative
knowledge is often present in much more down-to-earth situations: in such things as the activity of a child who takes a
clock apart to see how it works, or of a man chatting across the
back fence with a friend about the new family which has
moved into the neighborhood.

While the purposes grouped in these four categories are
plainly quite different from one another—and indeed, as we
shall see, cannot be reduced to one another or to some common denominator underlying them all—all do at least have
this much in common: it is possible to understand them without reference to the action of an agent seeking to realize
them. As purposes, their meaning is independent of human
action (which is not to say that they themselves have an independent existence, as if they were Platonic Ideas, but only that
the activity of someone trying to realize them is not included
in what they mean).

There is, however, another group of purposes which can
be sought for their own sake but whose meaning inherently
implies human action. Self-determining action is involved in
their very meaning. (Although the terminology is not especially important here, the purposes of the first kind can be
called "substantive" and those of the second "reflexive.")

All people experience tensions within themselves. The contemporary concern with "getting it all together" points to the
fact that people generally sense that they are *not* able to get it
all together—at least not permanently or to the degree they
wish. Different given aspects of the self seem continually at
war with one another, and the human response is to
struggle—more or less successfully for different persons at
different times in their lives—to resolve these tensions and
conflicts and achieve inner harmony. The objective sought is

integration of the aspects of the self. And this purpose is quite appropriately referred to as "integrity," in its basic meaning of wholeness.

A similar tension exists between the realistic insights of individuals and their actions. It is true that an action is the act of the person performing it, yet the action is something other than the actor. Conflict is possible here, too, a conflict expressed in such comments as "I wasn't really myself when I did that" or "If I had known then what I know now, I wouldn't have done it." This purpose we call "practical reasonableness."

Looking further beyond the self, it is evident that we experience tensions in our relationships with others, and we also seek in many ways to overcome these tensions and establish harmony between ourselves and other people. The purpose sought is "friendship." But the word has a very broad meaning here. In popular parlance friendship is used only to describe the relationship of persons who know and like one another. As a basic purpose or good, however, friendship encompasses many other things: for example, justice and peace among individuals and groups, even the harmonious relationship between entire nations. In this extended sense one could say that, ideally, friendship is the fundamental purpose of an organization like the United Nations.

Finally, in this group of reflexive purposes one moves beyond relationships among people to consider the relationship between human beings and God. It may be objected that we are now entering the realm of theology or that we are assuming the existence of God. That, however, is not our intention. We do not presume either to demonstrate or to take for granted that God exists.

For our purposes, what is significant here is simply the fact that, whether or not God exists, human beings in all cultures and in all times have been concerned about their relationship with a transcendent Other to whom the name "God" is usually

Integrity?

given. This concern has focused either on the attempt to rees-
tablish a harmonious relationship with the Other (it being
believed or felt the relationship had been disrupted in some
way) or to strengthen and perfect this relationship where it
exists. This category of purposes can be labeled "religion," ③
and the many different things done by many different people
in many different cultures in the attempt to restore harmony
between themselves and the transcendent Other (however
understood) are all directed to a religious good.

At this point the question very legitimately arises, Is this
all? Does this list of goods—life, play, aesthetic experience,
and speculative knowledge; integrity, practical reasonableness, friendship, and religion—exhaust the categories of purposes which can be sought for their own sake? It seems so.

Anyone, of course, can identify many more purposes than
these—purposes which to particular individuals or particular
cultures seem or have seemed far more important than any of
the ones listed here. Upon examination, though, it becomes apparent that such other purposes are actually no more than
aspects or combinations of aspects of these fundamental
goods. The fact that they may seem more important to an
individual or a group simply reflects the choices which have
been made within the limits of the cultural conditioning or
psychological inclination of that individual or group.

Historically, for example, particular societies have placed
their major emphasis on a good such as patriotism and have
made it their supreme purpose. But "patriotism"—a word
describing the relationship of mutual loyalty and support of
individuals in the same country—is no more than a limited
aspect of the broader category of goods we have called
"friendship."

Again, an individual may say that the basic goal of his or
her life, the purpose which gives everything else meaning, is
some such good as self-fulfillment. But, as we saw in chapter
four, fulfillment, although in a very general sense what gives

meaning to human life, is in practice a blanket term which means different things to different people and is in any case made up of various aspects of the goods we have described here.

In short, these eight goods seem to comprise all of the fundamental purposes of human action. Any other purpose either will include a bit of some or all of them or will represent a limited aspect of some of them. Wherever there is choice, one or another of the basic goods is somehow its object.

2. Are All Purposes Equal? Yes, but...

But while other purposes are reducible, in one way or another, to the purposes we have been describing here, these eight purposes are not reducible to one another, nor can they be reduced to a common denominator: some ultrafundamental, bedrock purpose which underlies all the rest. It would make matters far simpler if there were such a common denominator, for in that case, whenever choice was necessary, one could simply determine on the basis of calculation which available option was best suited to realize the common denominator purpose in the particular situation, and then act accordingly.

As a matter of fact—and complexity—however, each of these eight fundamental purposes is, looked at from its own point of view, the most important. This is one of the things that can make the choice of action so difficult.

Possibly this sounds like a surprising statement. Is there then no hierarchy of values? In a sense there is, but not in the sense that one can rank these eight fundamental goods in a rigid order of importance.

Everyone has a rough hierarchy of values insofar as some purposes are more important to him or her than others, but this is a matter of subjective choice and temperament. Obviously, too, we often make the judgment that someone who, say, puts success ahead of honesty (who is willing to cheat and lie to get what he or she wants) has a false hierarchy of values; but this is based on our working assumption that dishonesty is immoral and that if one has to choose between being moral and being successful, one should choose to be moral.

All this is true enough, but we repeat what we said: There is no objective hierarchy of values among the eight fundamental goods we have been examining, because each in its own way is most important.

Someone may find this acceptable enough in regard to a purpose like life or religion, but a bit hard to swallow in the case of play. So let us take play and see how it can be called the most important value.

From its own point of view, play (as we have described it here—engaging in a performance simply because one enjoys the performance) is the most important thing in life. Several considerations make this clear. Most people, after all, spend most of their waking hours working more or less doggedly simply in order to have a little leisure in which to do what they want to do—in which, in other words, to play. Furthermore, unless people are occasionally able to get away from the necessary side of life and engage in play, no other purposes can fully open up to them.

This is true even in regard to religion. If there is in one's approach to religion no room for the notion of play—doing something beautiful for God simply because it is a fine thing to do—and if religion is a matter of strict quid-pro-quo necessity, then religion has been effectively debased by being reduced to a kind of deal with the transcendent (I will sacrifice my oxen in order to please the gods so that they will make the rain fall, etc.). For religion to be something more than a contractual relationship between oneself and the Other, there must be room for play in one's religious life.

One could run through the rest of the goods and see that the same is true of all of them. Life is most important because unless people live they lose the opportunity to realize any other purposes. Speculative knowledge is most important because unless people have a grasp of truth they live truncated, partial lives. Religion is most important because unless people are on satisfactory terms with God (the transcendent) nothing else really matters. And so on. Looked at from its own point of view, each fundamental purpose is most important.

This does not mean, however, that these purposes are not related to one another. As a matter of fact, integrity, practical reasonableness, friendship, and religion are so intimately related that, to the degree one fails to realize one of them, one also fails to realize them all. This is because each of these purposes involves, in a different way, the quest for harmony in life: harmony among aspects of the self, harmony between one's self and one's outward behavior, harmony between the individual and other people, and harmony between individuals and the transcendent Other whom we call God. It is a fact of experience that when any one of these relationships is disturbed, the other relationships are also affected and to a degree undermined.

Furthermore, these four purposes are related to the other four—life, play, aesthetic experience, and speculative knowledge—in the sense that the latter must serve as vehicles for the former. It is impossible to act simply to achieve integrity, practical reasonableness, friendship, or religion—and no more. Inevitably it is necessary to include in one's action one of the purposes from the substantive group in order to give content to the activity by which one seeks to realize a purpose from the reflexive group.

An example makes this clear. Consider friendship. One might say that one seeks to realize friendship by being friendly. True, but a friendly act must have some substance to it. If a young man and young woman go on a date together (a friendly act), the date has got to involve some sort of specific activity: taking a walk in the park (play), going to a concert or a movie (aesthetic experience), talking (speculative knowledge—with perhaps a bit of play or aesthetic experience thrown in), or whatever.

The reverse, however, is not true. Life, play, aesthetic experience, and speculative knowledge *can* be sought by themselves, without reference to integrity, practical reasonableness, friendship, or religion. To go back to an earlier example, the drowning man struggling to keep his head above water has just one end in view: saving his life. It is most unlikely that he is concerned at the moment with integrity, practical reasonableness, friendship, or even religion.

Another point worth emphasizing (and important, as we shall see later, for understanding how people choose wrongly) is that it is rather commonplace for persons to single out a particular aspect of a good and to act on behalf of it while disregarding other aspects of the purpose understood in its entirety. For instance, "feeling well" is part of the good of life and health, yet it is by no means unheard of for people to do things for the sake of "feeling well" which are in fact injurious to life and health viewed in a larger perspective. Similarly, "getting it together" and "feeling no pain" are aspects of the good of integrity or self-integration, but it is quite possible to do things in the name of "getting it together" which miss the fuller reality of self-integration understood as harmony among all the parts or elements of the self.

In listing and describing the eight fundamental purposes we do not mean to suggest that they already exist fully or even that, conceptually, they are fully determinate. Indeed, nobody can say definitively what is meant by life, play, integrity, friendship, and the rest, because they have never been fully realized and never can be.

Why not? Because these purposes constitute the outline of human possibility—the outlines of what it means to be a human being. And, as such, just as we cannot help but understand them to some extent (because they are part of us, because they sum up what it means to be what we are: human beings), so we can never fully comprehend what they mean because we never in our lives exhaust the fullness of what it means to be human.

No matter how deeply we explore any or all of these fundamental human purposes, there is always something beyond—some further possibility for realizing, within these eight categories, what human life is all about. The only way in which we can gain ever-deepening understanding of these goods is by dedicating ourselves to them and seeking their realization in our lives and the lives of others.

Since the fundamental human purposes sum up the possibilities of human personhood, they constitute the framework within which self-determination is possible. In some way every act of self-determination is directed to some aspect of one or more of these purposes. But not every self-determining choice is morally good, and we therefore have much further to go to establish workable criteria for determining what makes a choice good or bad in the moral sense. Next we shall consider what the first and most basic criterion for answering this question might be.

Questions for Review and Discussion

1. Why is working for money not one of the basic purposes listed in this chapter?

2. Many empirical psychologists would list such things as food, drink, oxygen, and so forth as basic needs. How does the position set forth here take into account the fundamental character of activity directed toward satisfying such needs?

3. Traditionally liberal education has been concerned with play, aesthetic experience, and speculative knowledge. But as education becomes available to a larger part of a population, it tends to become

less liberal and to concentrate more on vocational preparation. Why do you think this is so?

4. Can you develop a theory explaining why an interest in play, aesthetic experience, and speculative knowledge might have developed as human beings moved from more primitive to more civilized conditions?

5. By what principle are integrity, practical reasonableness, friendship, and religion differentiated from each other?

6. Do you know of any theories in psychology, ethics, or other fields that tend to define the ideal of the good human life in terms of one (or less than all) of the purposes distinguished here?

7. Acts done simply because they are morally virtuous have traditionally been considered ends in themselves. If this is correct, the moral virtues must be included in the scheme of basic purposes. Where would they be included?

8. It might be argued that you cannot act for any one of the goods in the second group of four—integrity, practical reasonableness, friendship, and religion—without to some extent tending to realize all of them. Can you think of reasons for or against such a position?

9. Discuss the problem of the hierarchy of values. In order to set up a definite hierarchy, there must be a single, definite principle of ranking. Why can't a principle like self-realization serve as this principle?

10. According to our thesis, integrity, practical reasonableness, friendship, and religion require life, play, aesthetic experience, and speculative knowledge as vehicles. Illustrate this idea by the example of a quest for international justice.

11. Using examples from history, show how one of the purposes—justice, for instance—can be definite enough to serve as an objective but also open-ended enough to permit the unfolding of new dimensions of meaning.

8: "Ought" Points toward Fullness of Being

Having examined the fundamental purposes for which it is possible to act, we have made some progress toward establishing guidelines for making moral judgments about action. But we have not yet answered the central question: What makes some actions good and others bad? This basic issue still confronts us.

Curiously enough, though, in everyday life people routinely and without difficulty make value judgments in areas other than morality. They spontaneously say that objects and experiences are "good" or "bad," that things have been done as they "ought" or "ought not" to have been done. Examining what is meant by such expressions when they are used in nonmoral senses will not immediately tell us what they mean when applied to moral questions, but it will give us insights to help us understand moral "good," "bad," and "ought."

1. Good and Ought, Bad and Ought Not

The meanings of the words "good" and "ought" (as of the words "bad" and "ought not") are closely related. Their relationship becomes clear when one looks at areas other than morality. In doing so, however, it is important to bear in mind that we are merely trying to learn what can be learned by analogy about the meaning of these words. As we shall see, they are used in many different contexts and in diverse senses. It is important not to slip into the error of appropriating a meaning from some other context (for example, the idea that "goodness" is equivalent to "health," "evil" to "sickness") and applying it simplistically to morality. We can learn *something* about the meaning of "good" and "bad" as moral concepts from this kind of exercise in analogy, but we certainly cannot learn everything.

A good car is one which does well what a car ought to do. Of course, different people have different ideas about what a car ought to do, and thus they may disagree on whether a particular car is good or not. One driver puts the emphasis on speed and judges that any car which cannot do 120 mph is not a good one. Another driver is looking for economy and concludes that only a car which gets thirty miles to the gallon is good. Such differences, however, are beside the point here—the point being that however an individual determines what a car ought to do, a good car for that person will be one which meets his or her particular standards of oughtness.

The same fact—that "good" is closely related to "ought"—is universally observable. A good argument is one which reaches its conclusion as an argument ought to reach it (although there can certainly be strong differences of opinion even about logic). A good diet is one which provides what a diet ought to provide (a healthy gourmet may see this in quite a different light from an overweight man concerned about his heart condition). A good father does what a father ought to do (different fathers certainly have different views about what that is).

All this points simply to the fact that while there is plenty of room for disagreement about what a car or a diet or a father ought to do, everyone who uses the words "good" and "ought" quite naturally understands that they are inseparable in meaning (as are their counterparts "bad" and "ought not"). This is not a moral judgment; we are not even dealing with morality here. It is simply a judgment that the good thing will be the thing as it ought to be.

What exactly is this judgment expressing? What do we mean by saying that the good thing is the thing which is as it ought to be? To answer that question, it is necessary first to take note of the fact that existing things are often incomplete. Part of their reality is still in the order of potentiality. They are *something*, certainly, but they are not yet everything they can be. They have not yet become all that they are capable of being.

Furthermore, the possibilities of actually existing things are not mere fictions. It is not a fiction to say that a child is capable of becoming an adult. The future adulthood of children is a real thing, even though it does not exist yet. Adulthood for a child is an entirely real possibility which the child has simply not yet reached and realized.

We are not, however, leading up to the conclusion that moral goodness means fulfilling one's possibilities, while moral badness is failure to do so. The matter is considerably more complicated than that.

After all, badness is as real a possibility as goodness. The car which one purchased in the hope and expectation that it would be a good car can turn out to be a lemon, constantly laid up in the shop for repairs. The child whom one raised to be a good person can turn out to be evil, and in so doing he or she is fulfilling possibilities in as real a way as would be the case if he or she were good. People who are cruel, who exploit others, who break down community, realize their potential to the extent that cruelty, exploitation, and the destruction of community were among the possibilities open to them. The mere realization of a possibility does not mean that a thing or a person is thereby good.

2. Being and Being More

Some theories of what it means to be morally good and morally bad say in effect that goodness is health and vice is disease. This is the explanation offered, for example, by the psychoanalyst Erich Fromm. It is not an adequate explanation, because it does not leave room for freedom of self-determination and, in ruling out this freedom, it rules out the whole moral question as well.

If, after all, vice is simply a form of disease, from which one suffers, but which one does not choose, then self-determination just does not enter into the picture; and activity which is not the result of self-determination is not moral action at all (that is, it is neither moral nor immoral; it is simply amoral). It is true that some people act viciously because they are diseased, but in such cases they are not acting immorally, even though they are acting viciously. Where freedom is lacking, one cannot properly call action either moral or immoral.

While it is not possible to accept literally the goodness-is-health-and-badness-is-disease theory, the notion does contain the kernel of an idea worth exploring. Both "health" and "disease" describe ways in which an organism can function. How do we distinguish between them? One way of describing health is to say it is that way of functioning which is compatible with and leads to functioning further and more fully, while disease is a way of functioning that interferes with and closes off other possible functions.

In the nature of things, disease makes an organism less capable of further functioning; if the disease is serious enough, it eventually makes the organism incapable of functioning at all because it ends in death. Health on the other hand is a condition in which the possibility of functioning is open, and the more healthy the organism is, the more capable of functioning it is. Thus what is good for the organism (health) is to live and live more fully, whereas what is bad (disease) is for it to live less fully and eventually not live at all.

A similar pattern exists in the area of thought and inquiry. In this field, too, we make value judgments by saying, for example, that a particular argument is "good" or "bad." This need not be a moral judgment at all. One can properly acknowledge a good argument for what one regards as a morally bad position, just as one may recognize a bad argument for something regarded as morally good.

Various criteria enter into the nonmoral judgment that an argument is good or bad. One thing demanded of a good argument is clarity: no one regards confusion as desirable. Another trait is certitude: it is considered desirable that an intellectual inquiry lead to a definite conclusion instead of losing itself in vague rambling. A third criterion is explanatory power: in natural science it is considered desirable that a hypothesis be able to account for additional phenomena rather than that a new hypothesis be required to explain a newly observed phenomenon. Finally, one desires consistency: a train of thought should hang together and its components should not contradict one another.

Why are these characteristics—clarity, certitude, explanatory power, and consistency—regarded as desirable? It is because when they are present, knowledge is able to continue to grow and expand, and new areas for investigation and further understanding can open up; whereas when they are absent, further growth in knowledge and understanding becomes impossible. Confusion, endless inquiries, the absence of unifying principles, inability to explain things, internal inconsistency—these block thought and hamper investigation. The process by which we acquire further knowledge is crippled. Thus, in the area of thought and inquiry the good is that which makes possible further growth in knowledge; the bad is that which frustrates and renders impossible further growth.

Much the same pattern is found in the fields of art and technology. Creativity in fine art refers not only to the successful exploration of the possibilities of a particular medium but to an exploration carried on in such a way as to point to the possibility of still further fruitful explorations to be carried on by artists who come after. From this perspective the most creative artists, masters like Mozart and Rembrandt, are those who significantly expand the borders of their art form. Lesser artists are those who for the most part operate within the confines of what has already been achieved in a particular genre or style: they come up to the mark but they do not exceed it. As for artistic failures, they do not achieve even what has already been achieved. If they are innovators, their innovations prove to be dead ends. If they belong to an established artistic school or tradition, their work is mere sterile imitation, repeating the outward form of previous works without their inner spirit and tending to set art on the path of retrogression.

In technology, too, creativity means the opening up of new possibilities for further development—the sort of thing achieved by an Edison. Efficiency is also regarded as desirable in these areas, and efficiency is good because it fulfills possibilities in a way that leaves open further possibilities. By contrast, stultification sets in when the creative spirit flags and investigators are unable to go beyond what has already been achieved. Inefficiency is likewise bad because it not only fails to set new standards but is a waste of resources—because, in other words, it tends unnecessarily to limit possibilities.

In all of these areas—health, intellectual activity, art, and technology—we value or regard as good that which leads to being and being more; we judge to be bad that which cuts off further possibilities and tends toward the restriction of being.

To be sure, this is very abstract language. But the abstractness is necessary in order to sum up what one observes repeatedly in concrete circumstances in many different areas of life. The good is on the side of that which promotes being and its expansion and fullness. The bad is on the side of that which limits and contracts being and eventually terminates in nothingness or nonbeing.

3. What about Morality?

We still have not arrived at an understanding of moral good and bad, but we are in the process. Up to now we have simply seen what in various fields and apart from morality is meant by such words as "good," "bad," and "ought." We have not discovered anything very surprising—only that, in very general terms, the good is that which preserves being and makes possible more being, while the bad is that which limits being and tends toward nonbeing.

It is reasonable to suppose that the same pattern is present in the area of morality, with adaptations required by its particular subject matter. The subject matter of morality is free, self-determined human action. If therefore what we have just said is correct, moral goodness will be found in a kind of human action which not only realizes a person's potential for free action but realizes it in a way which tends toward fuller realization. By contrast, moral evil will be a way of acting which also realizes the human potential for self-determined action but does so in a manner that closes off possibilities for further free, self-determined action.

This is very general indeed and scarcely enables us to determine whether a particular action is morally good or bad. Even at this very general level we must examine more closely what the principle we have just expressed means and why it is

plausible to regard it as the principle of moral good and evil.
Beyond that it will be necessary to see how the principle
can—if it is accepted as valid—be applied to concrete circumstances in order to make moral judgments about individual
actions.

Yet the fact remains that, tentatively at least, we now do
have a very general principle for discriminating between
moral good and evil. Moral good is that which fosters human
being and *being more,* human living and living more fully.
Moral evil is that which puts limits on human being and contracts human life.

Moral evil amounts to a kind of existential suicide; moral
goodness amounts to ever-increasing growth in the realization of one's possibilities as a human person. But what makes
such growth possible? In the next chapter we shall try to
answer that question.

Questions for Review and Discussion

1. Some have argued that good is the more basic concept; others,
that ought is more basic. We do not directly enter this argument. Do
you see why not?

2. If someone thinks of potentiality as nothing more than a way
of referring to actuality at some time in the future, he or she would
not be able to make sense of the theory outlined here. Can you think
of arguments for or against the position that when we say "X can,"
we mean something more than "X will, if certain conditions are
fulfilled"?

3. Some philosophers say that values are irreducible to facts—
"ought" is irreducible to "is"—while others say values are nothing but
a particular set of facts. How does the position outlined here resolve
this issue?

4. To what field does the concept of "health" belong? Biology?
Investigate the history of the concept and current attempts to define
it, and compare with our analysis.

5. Good and bad in the area of thought and inquiry are in the

province of logic. If you have already studied some logic, analyze what was done in your course with reference to the criteria for this area which we suggest.

6. Exemplify from the field of art and literary criticism the way in which originality is used as a criterion of quality in the fine arts and literature.

7. Compare our remarks about efficiency with definitions of it to be found in introductory works in economics.

8. Some propose self-realization or self-actualization as the moral ideal. This position is obviously related to ours. But for several reasons we avoid such a formulation. How is our formulation more complex?

9. It has been said that the most fundamental question in ethics is "Who makes the rules?" Criticize this formulation of the problem in light of the analysis proposed here.

10. In each of the fields discussed in this chapter the values involved lead to do's and don'ts, and the standards of what ought to be lead to negative evaluations of that which falls short of the standards. Does this mean that disciplines like hygiene or logic are essentially negative and restrictive? If our analysis is correct, would the same conclusion apply to ethics?

9: Two Ways of Choosing

"To be or not to be." Hamlet stated the problem well. Although he clearly had something else in mind, his words do neatly sum up the two fundamental kinds of choice which are possible: choice in favor of being and choice in favor of nonbeing. The question of choice is important at this stage of our discussion because it carries us forward in the task of identifying and understanding the criterion of moral good and evil.

Up to this point we have seen that the very notion of moral good and evil involves freedom of self-determination. Where there is no free choice, no self-determination, morality is not in question. We have also seen that in order to be possible, human actions must be for purposes. If there were such a thing as an absolutely purposeless act, it would not be what we mean by a human act, which is directed to the realization of some purpose or good.

Thus the criterion of moral good and evil must involve both of these elements: freedom and purpose. It will be concerned with self-determining action performed in view of purposes. This, however, is to say that the matter of establishing a criterion of moral good and evil involves the question of choice, for choice is inextricably linked both with freedom (where there is no possibility of choice, there is no freedom) and with purposes (where many purposes exist but not all can be realized, it is necessary to choose among them).

Here we should recall something noted earlier about purposes. Fundamental human purposes are not outside persons but inside, not "out there" but within us. They are aspects of ourselves and of those whom we care about, intrinsic human possibilities, which it is up to us to realize. In acting to realize one of these purposes, we are not acting to achieve something impersonal (although acting to achieve something outside ourselves may very well be instrumental to realizing a basic human good); rather, we are striving to bring into being a part of ourselves by participating—taking part—in the good toward which our action is directed.

Realizing fundamental human purposes is not like acquiring material possessions, although in particular cases acquiring possessions, or renouncing them, may be a means to the realizing of purposes. Rather, at bottom it is *self*-realization, a way of creating oneself by giving reality to aspects of the self which were previously only possibilities.

In the last chapter we saw that the meaning of the word "ought," when applied to morality, parallels (with due regard for morality's proper subject matter) its meaning in other areas. "Ought" generally points toward full, fuller, and fullest being. Thus the moral "ought" points toward full and fuller freedom of self-determination and, ultimately, to the fullest possible self-determination. But since "self-determination" is simply another name for realizing what it means to be a person, "ought" in the moral sphere points ultimately to an ideal of the fullest possible personhood. The moral "ought" is a kind of verbal road sign directing travelers to their full humanity realized through freedom of self-determination.

Expressions like "the fullest possible personhood" and "full humanity" are of course more than a little vague. And with good reason. They signify something which is *not* a well-defined goal extrinsic to the self. The morally good life is *not* defined in terms of any such goal, even though, as we shall see, one who is morally upright will have many goals and projects.

To be sure, we all have in the backs of our heads some more or less hazy notion of what "full personhood" means for us. Upon examination, however, it will be seen that the meaning is rather significantly different from one individual to another. Furthermore, in the nature of things the ideal for each of us will always be—and must always be—more or less unclear.

It is possible to set specific objectives for oneself—to become a carpenter or a lawyer, say—and then set about achieving them in an efficient manner. But it is very different when it is a question of realizing one's ideal of personhood, which is likely to encompass such things as being wise and loving and religious. Purposes like these are open-ended, and in practice we come to understand their meaning in our lives only by working it out through a process of self-realization extending over a lifetime. The specific meaning, the content as it were, of being a "loving" person was simply not the same for Albert Schweitzer as it was for Francis of Assisi; the specifics of being a "wise" person were not the same for St. Paul and for Aristotle. The fundamental purposes were and are the same, but there is no way of mapping out in advance the precise steps one will be called upon to take in achieving one's fullest possible personhood through the realization of these fundamental human purposes or of describing in detail what "fullest possible personhood" will come to mean for one along the way.

If it were otherwise—if there *were* a way of mapping in advance the steps to be taken in achieving one's fullest possible personhood—that could only be because "fullest possible personhood" was an objective of second-level action. In that case it would be a limited, definite objective extrinsic to oneself—which is absurd.

The fundamental human purposes, described in chapter seven, create the field within which self-determination is possible. Taken together, they sum up the possibilities of human personhood, so that there can be no act of self-determination which is not directed to some aspect of one or more of them.

But moral goodness plainly consists in something else than simply choosing to pursue a fundamental human purpose. This happens *every* time we choose, yet not all our choices are morally good. Moral goodness and evil therefore specifically concern the manner in which choices are made.

This does not mean—to anticipate an objection—that anything whatsoever can be chosen, provided only that it is chosen in the right way. As we shall see, some things simply cannot be chosen in a morally correct manner. But, as we shall also see, even in these cases the problem is, not with the purposes to which the choices are directed, but precisely with the relationship which choices of this kind have to other fundamental human purposes. The problem concerns the dynamics of choosing.

One might think of fundamental human purposes as if they were goods on display in a large department store. Shoppers—human beings trying to live their lives in a morally correct manner—confront a rich variety of excellent wares. Considered in themselves, all are worth choosing. Still, no one person can choose everything—or absolutely anything whatsoever. Responsible shoppers will take into consideration how much money they can afford to spend, whether the goods they select are appropriate for them in view of their particular life-styles, the impact of their decisions on other persons to whom they have obligations, and so forth. Plainly, too, they will not obtain goods by shoplifting or by starting fires in the basement so that they can loot the store undetected. Evidently, then, whether they shop well or badly depends on how they choose among many different goods and how they act on their choices.

The image leaves much to be desired. (If taken too literally, it could lead one to suppose that, contrary to all we have said, human goods are indeed "out there," extrinsic to persons, and also that they are the sort of concrete, specific entities which are appropriate objects of second-level action.) But it does at least underline a crucial point: Choice is central to morality. Furthermore, in reflecting on moral goodness and evil we are dealing with choices which are true exercises of freedom of self-determination. As we have seen, in such choices people open themselves to participation in goods; they do not limit themselves to specific objectives extrinsic to themselves. Therefore, people bent on realizing their personhood must leave themselves as open as they can to the fullest possible range of human goods. Since everything in the department store is good, it would be unreasonable in making particular purchases to act as if the things one did not choose were therefore worthless.

Thus, in making choices, as everyone must do, persons committed to the fullest realization of their personhood will chose in a way that leaves open the possibility of still further self-realization for themselves and others. Stated negatively, this means that as far as possible they will avoid making choices in a manner which cuts them off from the goods not chosen and locks them into a narrow and evermore restrictive pattern of personhood. They will choose in a way which, rather than obstructing growth, makes self-realization a process of lifelong growing.

1. Choice—Exclusivistic and Inclusivistic

We return now to the point at which we began: "to be or not to be." As far as choice is concerned, that sums up the available options: choice which permits further growth and choice which obstructs it.

One way of choosing can be called "exclusive" or, better perhaps, "exclusivistic." It may be objected that all choice is exclusivistic, since in choosing one thing a person naturally excludes the thing or things not chosen. But while this is certainly the case, it overlooks the significant fact that there are two radically different attitudes which one can bring to choosing.

First, in making a choice among alternatives one can choose in such a way—and with such an attitude—that those things which are not chosen are also not positively rejected. But, second, one's attitude can be such that the alternatives not chosen *are* rejected. The second way of choosing—with an attitude that positively rejects the alternatives not chosen— is what we mean by exclusivistic choice. Let us take a closer look at what it involves.

It is Sunday morning. You roll out of bed, turn off the alarm clock, and confront a choice: What to do this morning? There is nothing that you *have* to do; whatever you decide to do will be something you could choose for its own sake. There seem to be three possibilities: first, go out and buy the Sunday papers and spend the morning reading them; second, play tennis; third, go to church. Having thought the matter over, you decide to go to church. (We are, incidentally, not trying to advocate church-going; the example will work just as well if either of the other options is chosen.)

The question is: Having elected to spend the morning at church, how do you feel about reading the papers and playing tennis? If the choice has been made with an exclusivistic attitude, your state of mind now may be more or less as follows: "Who wants to read the papers anyway? All you get is bad news and ink on your fingers. It's a waste of time. And tennis? Knocking a ball back and forth is an occupation for nitwits. I can't see why anyone would even bother." So off you go to church, with a good conscience but a decidedly exclusivistic attitude.

Notice several things here. Before the choice is made, each of the three options—reading the paper, playing tennis, and going to church—is perceived as having value. You would find some meaning in doing any one of them. Since it is possible to do only one, however, you must choose among them. And in choosing one your attitude toward the other two undergoes a dramatic change. Abruptly, playing tennis and reading the paper, which originally seemed like good, satisfying ways of spending the morning, take on a negative cast. As options not chosen, they have become things to reject and disparage.

It is not enough now to leave them in the category of the not-chosen; it is necessary to cut them down to size by finding fault with them and, quite possibly, distorting the goodness of the option which was chosen (e.g., "Just think of all those sinners playing tennis this morning or lying in bed reading the Sunday papers, while I, virtuous soul that I am, am giving glory to God and good example to my fellows by going to church"). Before the choice each of the options had its own good about it, but after the choice only one—the option chosen—is still steadily seen as good, while the other two, subjectively at least, have been diminished in their goodness.

The same thing happens to one degree or another whenever one chooses exclusivistically. In doing so, people subjectively confine the good to what they have chosen, while downgrading the value of that in which they have elected not to share. They whittle down human possibilities to fit themselves and their limitations. Implicitly or explicitly they assert not only that what they choose has value but that it has superior value, and that the things they do not choose are *thereby* reduced in value. This means that implicitly or explicitly they deny that values are intrinsic human possibilities, which have value in themselves and which therefore keep their value even if an individual does not choose to act on their account in particular circumstances.

It is, however, also possible to choose with an inclusive—or, better, inclusivistic—attitude. This simply means that while choosing one alternative out of two or more, a person continues to respect the values which are present in the alternatives not chosen. One who chooses in this way in effect acknowledges his or her own limitations—no one can be or do everything—and does not shift the blame, as it were, onto the options-not-chosen by denying their value.

We can see more clearly what this means by returning to our example. Once again the choice is the same: to go to church instead of reading the papers or playing tennis. But this time the choice is made in an inclusivistic manner. What then is one's attitude toward the other two alternatives?

Quite simply, it is honest recognition that there is merit in both of them. Reading the papers is an informative and entertaining way to spend time; playing tennis is good exercise and a lot of fun. Neither has been chosen on this occasion, but one's appraisal of their value remains what it was before the choice; and this is exactly what it would have been if they had been chosen instead. All the options possess certain values. The fact that one has not chosen two of them is no reflection on either, but only an indication that nobody can read the papers, play tennis, and go to church simultaneously.

We ought always to choose inclusivistically. For consistent inclusivism in choice is the criterion of moral goodness we have been seeking, whereas moral evil consists in choosing exclusivistically. Indeed, it can be said that no one chooses precisely to *do what is morally wrong;* rather, one *makes choices in a way that is morally wrong*—in an exclusivistic manner. (This should not, however, be turned around, as if to say that choosing in a morally right manner makes whatever one chooses morally right. This is not so—there are some things which simply cannot be chosen with a right attitude—and we shall have much more to say about this below. Here we shall only say that as not even the best cook in the world can make a gourmet meal out of garbage, so no one can choose with a right attitude something which *cannot* be chosen with a right attitude.)

Upon reflection, it becomes apparent that inclusivistic choice corresponds to what we suggested earlier as the mean-

ing of moral "ought": the fullest possible realization of ourselves as free. When we choose inclusivistically, we remain
open to further self-realization even in directions we have not
chosen. Although we have chosen X instead of Y or Z, we
continue to acknowledge the good which made Y and Z interesting, and in doing so, we remain open to the possibility of
realizing that good at another time and given different circumstances. We have not closed off growth in any area of life
(which is to say, growth in ourselves).

By contrast, because it involves an attitude which denies
the full value of that which is not chosen, exclusivistic choice
not only forgoes self-realization in these directions here and
now but tends to block it in the future and permanently by
creating a mind-set which denies that there is goodness there
to be chosen. If, to return to our example for a moment, one
has once persuaded oneself that reading the paper or playing
tennis is valueless, one has by that very fact made it at least a
bit more difficult—and possibly a great deal more difficult—
ever to engage in those activities (and thereby realize the values involved in them) in the future. In this way one has narrowed the dimensions of one's own personhood.

2. The Meaning of Immorality

The truth of what has just been said becomes more clear
when it is seen that the criterion of moral evil outlined here
fits the various meanings of the word "immorality." When we
call something immoral, we are saying that it is a kind of
self-mutilation, that it represents unreasonableness in action,
that it is a violation (at least incipient) of community, and that
it is a rejection of the transcendent Other, God.

First, self-mutilation. When we are confronted with a
choice, each alternative corresponds to something within us
reaching out to be realized. In any choice among alternatives,

of course, something goes unrealized. But in exclusivistic choice the aspect of the self which is not realized is suppressed and denied. It is told in effect not only that it cannot be realized here and now but that it should not be realized, because it is not reaching out to any value. When we do this, a part of our personality dies a little; if it happens often enough, it may die entirely.

Second, unreasonableness in action. In order to see the options in a choice situation as real alternatives, we must take for granted that each has some genuine value or goodness. Before the choice is made, we hear the appeal made by the value in each of them. But in choosing exclusivistically (acting immorally) we not only decline to respond to the appeal of the alternatives not chosen; we must also refuse to hear the appeal—must deny that there is anything to hear. In doing so, however, we deafen ourselves to an appeal to which nobody can possibly be deaf, because it comes from within oneself. It is necessary to deny the reality of that of which we are perhaps all too aware because it is part of us. To put this point in a more literal and abstract way: A person who chooses exclusivistically treats as not-good what is not chosen, but what is not chosen had a *chance* to be chosen only because the person recognized it as a good. Herein lies a kind of inconsistency which is not logical contradiction but which is unreasonableness in action.

Third, violation of community. When we choose exclusivistically, we are saying in effect that the alternatives not chosen are without value. If, then, someone else confronted with the same alternatives makes a different choice, it follows that he or she has chosen what is worthless. And presumably an individual who chooses what is worthless is either stupid or perverse. Thus exclusivistic choice inherently creates a situation of conflict between the individual who chooses in this way and others who make different choices; whereas one who chooses inclusivistically, because he or she continues to recognize the value in what is not chosen, is also able to acknowledge the reasonableness and decency of others who make different choices and to appreciate the enrichment of the human community brought about by the very fact of difference.

Fourth, rejection of God. Immoral action is also called sinful or antireligious. A genuinely religious attitude acknowledges that human purposes and possibilities have meaning which transcends the particular significance they have for the individual—meaning related in some way to the transcendent Other whom we call God. However, when we choose in an exclusivistic manner, we assert in effect that the good is simply that which we choose, and "goodness" means no more than what we cause it to mean by choices. By contrast, inclusivistic choice leaves us open to the possibility that the meaning of goodness and the meaning of our own lives are not limited to whatever arbitrary content we give them but do in fact derive at least partly from their relation to something or someone transcendent. Exclusivistic choice denies that goods which are not chosen have any higher principle which sustains them as good even when they are not chosen; inclusivistic choice affirms (in an implicit way, usually) the reality of transcendent support for human possibilities.

It bears noting, finally, that inclusivistic choice involves an attitude of service to, rather than domination of, the goods or purposes of human life. People who choose in this way are not imposing their vision on reality; rather, they acknowledge goodness where it exists and seek to realize it to the best of their ability even while admitting that because of their own limitations, they cannot realize every possible human purpose in their own lives. This mode of choice thus corresponds to the third level of action which, as we have seen, basically involves the realization of human goods through participating in them.

If, however, we regard the alternatives in a choice situation in such a way that not choosing something transforms it by removing the value which it previously possessed (exclusivistic choice), from then on in regard to that good we are involved only in action at the second level. For this implies that a thing has goodness only insofar as it is a concrete objective and that if we choose not to seek and possess it, it ceases to have value.

This is the paradox—the irrationality in action—of exclusivistic choice, seen now from another point of view. We set out to make a free choice, to exercise self-determination; we end up pursuing a particular objective, our action now merely a matter of doing as we please. Instead of realizing his or her self by remaining open to fuller personhood, the person choosing exclusivistically makes even that aspect of the self which is fulfilled by the choice a definite and limited objective, which is now *extrinsic* to the very center of his or her personhood. In choosing exclusivistically one moves from *being a person* to *having something* one happens to want.

This is not to say that it is impossible to act immorally at the third level. Quite the contrary. For the point is precisely this: Immoral action could well be described as third-level action which consists in choosing to place oneself at the second level—and stay there. Later we shall see more of what this means.

Questions for Review and Discussion

1. One reason some people take a subjectivist position is that they are afraid of an externally imposed morality—one which would make morally good action into second-level action. Discuss the way in which the theory outlined here reconciles objectivity with freedom.

2. Is inclusivism itself exclusivistic inasmuch as it excludes its opposite?

3. In what sense can one choose to do what is morally wrong?

4. Think of examples of actions which you consider morally evil but in which you can nevertheless find the good for which the action might be done. How must a person who resists temptation proceed if he or she is to choose inclusivistically?

5. Discuss the difference between self-mutilation and self-restraint. Do you know of any theories of moral development that confuse the two?

6. What is the difference between the rationality of action demanded here and the consistency that even a subjectivist theory requires?

7. Some theories of ethics hold that the morally good is what builds up community, while the morally bad is what harms others. Distinguish the criterion of morality proposed here from such alternative theories.

8. Some religious theories of morality reduce moral goodness to obedience to divine commands. William of Ockham, a fourteenth-century theologian, went so far as to say that if God commanded us to do just the opposite of what the Ten Commandments say, we would be morally obliged to do so. How does our view of immorality as rejection of God differ from religious theories of that sort?

9. The theory proposed here rejects the idea that in choice we create or transform values. How, then, can it be said that in this theory there is room and need for creativity in moral life?

10. If immoral action occurs at the third level, it must be directed toward at least a partial and mutilated aspect of one of the eight categories of fundamental human purposes discussed in chapter 7. In which category do you think the good lies to which immoral acts are directed?

10: The Ethics of Love

Advocates of the new morality who have followed the discussion up to now are very likely in a highly exasperated state. "What is all this talk about levels of action, categories of goods, inclusivistic and exclusivistic choice? What does this have to do with morality? There is no need to make an elaborate production out of moral judgment—and all your jargon merely obscures what is in reality perfectly simple. The moral criterion is love. If people act lovingly, they act morally. That's the long and the short of it."

Would that it were so simple! Several different ethical theories are embraced under the headings of the "new morality" or "situation ethics," but none provides an adequate account of human action or the standard by which moral judgments are to be made. And to say "It's all a matter of loving and acting lovingly" turns out upon examination to be no more than a source of confusion at best and, at worst, an excuse for shirking the hard work of judging and acting morally.

1. Relatives and Absolutes

One theory encompassed under the heading "new morality" or "situationism" is the moral relativism of John

Dewey. His is a rather pure version of the situationist ethic, which holds that there are no absolute values: all values are relative to a particular situation. The value of values, one might say, is determined by the situation, not by anything inherent in the values. This view is founded on a false understanding of the reality of a moral situation. It assumes that, morally speaking, the situation is something given, which imposes morality on us. In reality the reverse is true.

The situation does not impose morality on us; we impose morality on the situation. The moral dimension becomes present according to the manner in which we perceive the facts of the situation and respond to them through free, self-determining choices.

We have made this point earlier, but it is worth returning to it here in the context of our discussion of the new morality, the "love is everything" ethic. To illustrate what we are saying, let us take one of the most controverted moral issues of recent times, the Vietnam war, and consider the appropriate response of individuals called on to participate in that war.

Leaving aside all passionate rhetoric, there were only two judgments one could make about participation in the war in Vietnam: it was moral or it was immoral. Now let us imagine two draft-eligible young men—John and Steve—faced with induction in 1968, at the height of American ground involvement. Let us also suppose that both young men were in possession of the same factual information about the war, but that John had made previous choices by which he had made himself especially sensitive to the threat of Communism, whereas Steve's prior choices made him more concerned about the value of human life. What was the moral situation confronting these two young men?

For John the situation was this: South Vietnam, a small, peaceful country friendly to the United States, had for all practical purposes been invaded by aggressive, Communist North Vietnam. The United States, prompted by altruism, had gone to the aid of the aggressor's victim. It was a classic case of a Good Samaritan stepping in to protect the weak from being victimized by the strong. John accepted induction into the army willingly, convinced that it was right for him to do so.

For Steve the situation was this: two factions of Vietnamese were contesting for control of their country. The United States, blinded by anti-Communist zealotry and anxious to retain its strategic foothold in Southeast Asia, had intervened on behalf of the military dictatorship heading one of the factions. Its intervention had been unusually violent, resulting in widespread loss of civilian life. The war was immoral and the United States had no right to be involved in it. Steve refused induction into the army, convinced that it was right for him to do so.

Our purpose is not to argue the morality of the Vietnam war. It is to illustrate that the moral situation created by the war could and did appear very different to different people, not because of different information but because of different precommitments. And as a result of their different perceptions of the situation, different people responded in very different ways.

If situationism were correct, this could not have happened: the situation would have forced the response on individuals. But in fact just the opposite occurred. Individuals in effect created the moral situation for themselves on the basis of their preconceptions and their understanding of the facts. In saying that the morality of a situation is given by the situation itself, situationists are only saying that preconceptions often cause people to perceive particular situations in a certain way, so that they are no longer interested in taking another look—either at their perceptions or at their preconceptions—to determine whether they square with reality: "Don't confuse me with facts." It is true that people do often act in this way, but that does not constitute the basis for a true and viable ethical theory.

2. Utilitarianism

Also embraced under "new morality" is the theory of utilitarianism, which received its classic statement in the works of Jeremy Bentham and, especially, John Stuart Mill. Basically, utilitarianism holds that when a choice must be made, the morally right thing to do is to choose the alternative which will result in the greatest net good or, if all the alternatives will have adverse consequences, in the smallest net harm.

Bentham equated goodness with pleasure. But this was soon seen to be a faulty explanation because it leads logically to the conclusion that, for example, a happy pig is in a more fortunate condition than Socrates. Mill improved the theory by arguing that the good involved is the greatest happiness for the greatest number of people and by further recognizing that it is not just the quantity of pleasure or happiness which is important but its quality.

Utilitarianism, however, necessarily involves a number of grave difficulties which render it unacceptable as an ethical theory. For one thing, to suppose that the moral criterion is the greatest good or happiness for the greatest number of people is, as even Bentham and Mill correctly recognized, to make morality a matter of quantitative measurement. This in turn demands that there be a common denominator of goodness or happiness—that all purposes or values be ultimately reducible to the same thing, so that, as required by the theory, they can be measured by the same yardstick. Bentham bluntly suggested that a monetary value should be assigned to everything in which any human person is interested.

We have seen that fundamental human purposes cannot be reduced to a common denominator without adopting some such arbitrary procedure. Each is the most important from its own perspective. None is objectively reducible to another, nor are all reducible to some ultrafundamental superpurpose underlying all. This rules out merely quantitative measurement in moral matters.

Indeed, this is implicit even in Mill's own recognition of qualitative differences among goods and pleasures. To recognize qualitative differences introduces a fatal flaw into utilitarianism, although at the same time it opens the door to a more plausible understanding of morality. Mill was quite right in acknowledging that enjoyments—goods, pleasures, purposes—are qualitatively different. But precisely because they are, there is and can be no common denominator, no universal measuring rod, of the sort which would be imperative if utilitarianism were to be a viable ethical system. Thus utilitarianism turns out to be a dead-end street, an illustration from the field of ethics of the futility of trying to add apples and oranges—or, better, of trying to say which is larger: the number 756 or the length of a rainbow.

It should of course be noted that an exact calculation of the net good and evil consequences of action, as envisioned by utilitarianism, is possible, but only at the second level of action, where one acts to achieve concrete, limited goals. In effect, the theory seeks to determine the success or failure of action in achieving specific objectives.

We emphasize again, as we have before, that this way of acting—and calculating—is an altogether necessary and proper part of life. But morality, as we have also emphasized, is basically concerned with self-realization through third-level action: action by which one determines one's self through participation in fundamental human purposes or goods. Calculation of the kind presupposed by utilitarianism is simply impossible at this level of action, because the values or purposes involved are not embodied in a set of specific external objectives to be achieved but are instead aspects of one's own personhood to be realized through the process of self-realization.

At bottom, utilitarianism amounts to telling people to act in order to achieve what is good without answering the question of what is good. If it assumes that every kind of goodness is fundamentally the same as every other kind, so that all can be weighed on the same scale, it assumes what is untrue. If it acknowledges that there are different kinds of goods which are not reducible to a common denominator, it is correct; but in doing so it also rules out the kind of calculation about means and ends which alone would make utilitarianism workable.

3. Love Is/Isn't Everything

Other objections can easily be added to the list of criticisms of utilitarianism/new morality/situation ethics. What really is the situation in question? Typically, situationists include in their analysis only as much of a particular situation as happens to suit their purpose.

Consider the "situation" involved in dropping atomic bombs on Hiroshima and Nagasaki. The usual defense of this action—a utilitarian argument—is that it saved lives by hastening the end of Japanese resistance. If the situation is considered in this very narrow framework, the conclusion seems logical and the atomic-bombing of the two cities was a moral action. It is equally logical, however, to take into consideration other consequences (the killing of civilians, the unloosing of a new and particularly horrible instrument of violence, and so forth) and arrive at the opposite conclusion: this action was immoral. In situationism the one who defines the situation also and automatically determines the moral verdict.

Again, in telling us to act in a way that will bring about the most good for the largest number of people, the new morality offers little guidance as to which people it has in view. Does this apply only to people who have been born? It makes a considerable difference: for example, in determining the morality of abortion (where most advocates of the new morality would exclude the unborn from consideration) or in

judging the morality of proposals for building possibly
accident-prone nuclear energy plants (where many support-
ers of the new morality, adverting to the danger of genetic
damage from radiation, would reverse direction and include
unborn future generations in their moral calculation).

Despite its contradictions and inconsistencies, however, the
new morality has a powerful appeal today, particularly when
it employs the attractive slogan that "love alone is the standard of morality." Who, after all, can be against love?

Yet those who argue that love is all do not sufficiently
consider the enormous ambiguities involved in the use of the
word. Just which love are we speaking of here? In one sense
all people love themselves and others, and always act out of
love. The difference between a moral and an immoral dispo-
sition does not concern whether one loves and acts on the
basis of love; it concerns *how* one loves. Presumably the public
executioner loves the condemned man, but it makes a considerable difference whether—and why—the executioner does
or does not kill him.

In another sense love is a sentiment, a feeling. Happily, it is
a feeling which almost everyone experiences at some time or
other in life and perhaps at many times. But the experience of
being in love has nothing directly to do with morality, even
though it can well prove the point of departure for moral
goodness.

When we look into our own loves, we find not one love but
many. Each makes a more or less plausible claim to get its way
by controlling our choices and actions, but in fact our diverse
loves are more or less in conflict with one another. People love
their country and they also love their own lives. Are they,
therefore, acting morally or immorally in risking their well-
loved lives to defend their well-loved country?

This conflict of loves within us is the beginning of the
moral problem. If we had only one, dominant love, we would
never have to ask ourselves the question "What is my true

responsibility?" But because conflicting loves make conflicting claims upon us, we must wrestle with moral problems. We are forced to seek a standard for making moral judgments, and this seeking is the beginning of ethics. To say "Follow love" is not an ethics at all but a refusal to take ethical problems seriously.

There is nevertheless a kernel of truth in the love-ethic which lends it attractiveness. If we were perfectly good—if, that is, we loved in a fully open and generous way all of the goods that together make up the human person, and if our whole personality were integrated in harmony with this attitude, and if, further, we lived among other people who were just like us in this—then (and only then) would we not need any criterion of morality beyond our own inclinations.

"Follow love" would then make perfect sense, because our love would be a perfectly reliable moral guide. Confronted with alternatives, we would always make the morally right choice because nothing wrong (disordered, unbalanced, exaggerated) would have made any inroads in us. We would in fact "sense" what was right, much as healthy people sense without reflection the appropriate movements and responses necessary to keep their balance. This, in sum, is the meaning of St. Augustine's often quoted and almost as often misunderstood words "Love God and then do what you will."

Unfortunately, none of us seems yet to have arrived at such a state of perfection. Some are closer to it; some, further from it; none is there yet. For those of us whose love is more or less imperfect, the advice to follow love only amounts to saying "Do what you please." Many rationalizations can be found— not infrequently couched in idealistic terms—for doing what one pleases. But in the end, to do what one pleases is to do what one pleases. It is not an ethical position; it is ethical nonsense and moral chaos.

If we are to act morally, we need moral guidelines. Thought is admittedly a weak instrument in this area, but it is the only one we have. Without falling into the trap of supposing that our love *is* perfect, we must ask ourselves what we would do if our love *were* perfect. This is the ethical question, the answers to which will make it possible to develop sound ethical rules for living our lives. Next we shall examine the question and its answers in some detail.

Questions for Review and Discussion

1. John Dewey says situations present problems: felt evils to be dealt with. What is presupposed by the perception of a set of facts as evil?

2. Utilitarianism is based on the application of a technical model to human action: it amounts to thinking of all human action as if it were second-level action. How does this sort of theory have a legitimate application?

3. Why do you suppose such a theory as utilitarianism became so popular in the last century and this one?

4. Using situation ethics, think of opposite decisions that might be made on the morality of important current issues. Show how either decision, once made, can be given a plausible utilitarian justification.

5. Is it possible for the same person consistently to hold to subjectivism and utilitarianism in ethics?

6. Distinguish and exemplify as many different senses of "love" as you can.

7. Explain what is involved in the ideal case of perfect love. Do you think anyone ever approaches or has ever approached this ideal? Are there instances in your own experience in which your love of the good was sufficient to make you see the right thing to do—and do it—without even asking yourself what was the "right" thing?

8. Authors who advocate situation ethics often use examples involving sexual morality. Can you think of any reason why they should concentrate on examples from this field?

9. Some advocates of situation ethics claim that it is Christian morality and that for Christians the only moral absolute is the demand to do what love requires. How does this square with your reading of the New Testament?

11: Guidelines for Love

Moral rules do not enjoy an especially good reputation today. The preceding chapter suggests why. A state of affairs in which moral rules are necessary is less than ideal, and today many people wish to make a dramatic leap into the ideal. Yet it remains a disconcerting fact that human beings seem to be something other than ideal—in which case moral rules are necessary. People with 20/20 vision do not need eyeglasses, but those with imperfect vision find them a necessity. Morally speaking, we all have imperfect vision. Moral rules help us to compensate for this imperfection and to see more clearly what we ought to do.

In other words, to see more clearly means in this case to know with some degree of exactness what our concrete moral responsibilities are. In what follows we are not attempting to provide a moral handbook, a neat summary of common moral responsibilities. The concrete responsibilities of each individual are different, and it is these which are important. We cannot tell individuals what their responsibilities are, and we would not wish to take on such a task even if it were possible.

What we shall try to do instead is to provide assistance for individuals who wish to think through their own lives and come to a better understanding of their responsibilities. As we have seen, the basic principle of morality is: One ought always

111

to choose inclusivistically. The question is, How does this basic principle take shape in each individual person's unique body of moral responsibilities?

The moral guidelines we shall discuss do not, as we have said, comprise a handbook of common responsibilities. They might instead be described as general principles from which each person can develop his or her own detailed moral code; they are also principles by which any existing or possible moral code can be evaluated. Since these principles shape and control moral responsibilities, we call them "modes of responsibility." We shall deal with six such modes in this chapter; two others of extreme importance and complexity will receive separate treatment in the chapters that follow.

The modes of responsiblity are not our arbitrary invention: they are rooted in the fundamental human goods or purposes and the general moral principle we have already examined. This is to say that they are not extrinsically imposed rules but are part of the intrinsic structure of the moral life we are seeking to uncover and reflect upon. Nor are these modes of responsibility something apart from or over against human beings. Rather, just as the fundamental goods are goods of persons, so the modes of responsibility constitute intelligible requirements for realizing these goods in and for persons, ourselves and others.

What we have just said bears amplification. Up to this point we have identified the fundamental human goods which, taken together, constitute the possibilities of human personhood. We have also identified the first and basic principle of morality: choose inclusivistically—which is to say, choose in a way that leaves one open to ever-fuller realization of the fundamental goods which are constitutive of one's personhood. Now, however, we need moral principles which will specify this first principle by ruling out certain kinds of actions involving a relationship to the human goods other than that required by the first principle itself. It is these which we call modes of responsibility.

Moral philosophers have sometimes mistaken one or another of the modes of responsibility for the first principle of morality. It is a natural enough mistake, since the modes of responsibility are specifications of this principle. Still, the first principle is broader than any one or several of these modes; in order to achieve consistent observance of the first principle, we must take all the modes of responsibility into account and choose in a manner consistent with them all.

Now let us see what these modes of responsibility are.

1. Consistent Commitments

To begin with, if an individual's attitude toward all the fundamental human purposes is open and inclusivistic (the basic criterion of moral goodness), he or she will not live for passing satisfactions or for specific future objectives. An individual of this sort will instead be committed to the realization of basic purposes with which he or she can identify to such an extent that the free actions by which they are realized will in fact constitute him or her as a person. Furthermore, such a person will make a number of such commitments: large, third-level actions like marrying or engaging in a profession. And, further still, an individual of this sort will strive to make commitments consistent with one another, so that they form a harmonious framework for life. This, then, is the first mode of responsibility: consistent commitment to a harmonious set of purposes or values.

The consistency involved here is not consistency over a period of time, which, although also important, is more a matter of fidelity. What is in question is instead the internal consistency of a person's commitments and purposes, of which it may be said, when consistency is present, that they "hang together" in an integrated way. This state of affairs is not necessarily the outcome of highly sophisticated introspection. Quite simple people are as capable as others of the requisite consistency, which is achieved by—and reflected in—making long-range choices (such as marriage, work, etc.) in a responsible and prudent manner. To do this one does not have to think deep thoughts about The Meaning of It All, and, indeed, some of those who do—people, that is, who seem more taken up with abstractions than with the practical requirements of ordering and conducting their lives—are quite unsure about just who they are.

Negatively, this mode of responsibility rules out a certain kind of premoral spontaneity, in which persons put themselves at the service of desires or inclinations not harmonized with the rest of their fundamental life-purposes. Many people do in fact spend a great part of their lives in the service of such goals—pleasure, wealth, status, and so forth—which do not represent rational commitments but instead originate as mere wants or cravings. Such unreflective, slavish activity is altogether inappropriate in a life of free self-determination.

At the same time there is a place for spontaneity within morality. For the individual who has integrated his or her commitments into a consistent pattern, spontaneous action within this pattern can become almost second nature. But spontaneity in this case is in line with commitments, not something which precedes commitment. From the perspective of this mode of responsibility, immorality consists in using mature powers in the service of infantile goals, while morality means organizing life around basic commitments and acting within the pattern created by this organization.

2. The Golden Rule

A second mode of responsibility is reflected in the fact that if one has an open and inclusivistic attitude toward all the fundamental human purposes, one will at all times take into account all of the goods and will, furthermore, do so not merely as they apply to oneself but as they apply to all other human beings. People with this attitude do not regard themselves as special cases, demanding concessions and favors they are unwilling to grant to others. They regularly ask themselves "How would I like it if somebody did this to me?"—which is another way of putting the thought expressed in the classic formulation of the Golden Rule: Do unto others as you would have them do unto you.

Clearly, this mode of responsibility is violated frequently in ordinary experience. Violations are especially common on the part of people who have undergone a change in their state of life and no longer remember how things looked "on the other side." How many parents, for example, inflict injustices on their children which they, as children suffering the same injustices at the hands of *their* parents, vowed never to be guilty of in adult life!

3. Openness

A third mode of responsibility, also involving relationships with others, might be described simply as openness: willingness to help others, desire to see them develop and perfect themselves by realizing to the fullest the goods of which they are capable. A person with this attitude is not defensive or selfish about protecting his or her own position of excellence or superiority in relation to others.

A striking example is provided by the good teacher who genuinely rejoices in seeing students progress in their particular skill or discipline, even if the students in time come to outshine the teacher. People with this attitude will also accept and take satisfaction in the ways in which others are different from them: they will not demand that everyone mirror their own tastes and enthusiasms.

From the viewpoint of this mode of responsibility, morality is often expressed in willingness to accept responsibility for the needs of another even when no structured relationship with the other compels one to do so. Conversely, immorality is apparent in the actions of persons who feel no responsibility for others with whom they come into contact in unstructured relationships (e.g., the driver who does not stop or send help back to a stranded motorist). To insist on having a clear-cut duty before doing what is necessary to help someone else reflects an immoral attitude.

4. *Detachment*

Detachment is the word which characterizes a fourth mode of responsibility. Its contrary is manifested by people so oriented toward one purpose that its frustration or loss is a shattering experience which drains their lives of meaning. A person with a morally good attitude, an openness to all human goods, will not be so totally destroyed by the loss, no matter how genuinely painful, of any one of them. Put in terms of levels of action, the fourth mode of responsibility means that one should never regard the specific and limited objective of a second-level action as if it were itself the human good to which one is committed and in which one participates through a third-level action.

A person with a religious turn of mind may object that what has just been said may apply to most things, indeed almost all, but cannot apply to loving God above all else, for that is something to which every human being ought to be totally and uniquely dedicated. A Jew or Christian can hold that this is true, so long as he or she keeps in mind that God is not an aspect of the human personality, that God transcends all human goods, and that humankind is made in God's image, so that each human good is a partial reflection of God's infinite goodness and lovability. These things assumed, one should conclude that, properly understood, the love of God implies love for all human goods: implies, in other words, precisely the morally good attitude which we have been attempting to describe. However, it *is* possible to overidentify with and overcommit oneself to the human good of religion, in which case the aberration is what is called religious fanaticism.

5. Fidelity

The fifth mode of responsibility complements detachment. While prepared to accept the loss of particular satisfactions and achievements without regarding this as a final loss of their personhood, people should nevertheless remain committed to their ideals: they should practice fidelity. A person with such an attitude will persist in seeking to realize realistically realizable purposes; by contrast, a person without it will tend to give up rather easily upon encountering problems and obstacles.

Fidelity or stability in commitment to purposes is not the same thing as mere constancy, much less rigidity. It is dynamic, implying continuing effort to explore new ways of better serving the purposes to which one is committed. It also involves refusal to narrow down a human good to those particular expressions of it with which one happens to be familiar. A creative and open approach to living is not only consistent with fidelity but essential to it.

Put in terms of levels of action, this fifth mode of responsibility—fidelity—means that one should never regard the human goods to which one is committed and in which one participates through free, self-determining acts at the third level as merely the specific, limited, extrinsic objectives of second-level actions.

Detachment and fidelity balance each other in the lives of individuals. They enable people to strike a mean between the immoral extremes of fanaticism and noninvolvement. They also rule out an attitude of unwillingness to attempt difficult things and thereby risk failure.

Morality does not require that one take needless risks or be unrealistic about circumstances, including one's own abilities, and the consequent chances of failing in an undertaking. But persons with a morally good attitude will be inclined to push beyond what they and others have already accomplished and to take reasonable chances in the process, aware that many good things in life will never be done except by people who are willing to run the risk of failing in the attempt.

6. *Pursuit of Limited Objectives*

Under the sixth mode of responsibility one will seek specific ends which truly contribute to the realization of the broader, deeper purposes to which one has dedicated one's life. The pursuit of specific objectives which can be attained by definite, limited means should always be included within the framework of our basic self-constitution.

This may seem a surprising thing to say in view of the many critical comments we have made about the pursuit of limited objectives. Yet we have been careful also to balance these comments by pointing out that the pursuit of limited objectives plays a necessary, proper, and good role in the moral life. It is wrong to limit one's morality, and one's life, merely to this. But, provided life is grounded upon and built around commitment to a consistent set of purposes, it is not only good sense but one's responsibility to put flesh, as it were, on the bones of commitments by pursuing specific, limited ends which really do further their realization.

In many cases it is difficult to further the realization of a good, but it is possible and easy to gain an illusory experience of participating in it. For example, genuine self-integration is hard to achieve, but a temporary experience of inner harmony can be obtained easily by the use of alcohol or other drugs. If one knowingly chooses such an experience as a substitute for the effort necessary actually to further realization of the good, then the appearance becomes the enemy of the reality. Such choice is but one way—though a very widespread and significant way—in which this mode of responsibility can be violated. A truly good person takes more rational and effectual means of seeking ends to which he or she is committed.

Thus a person with a morally good attitude will try to be efficient and in a sense will live by the utilitarian code, although not *alone* by the utilitarian code: where there is no other moral issue, act to achieve the most good or to avoid the most harm.

Of course, one who is genuinely a utilitarian assumes that there never is any other moral issue: that is, that the moral value of alternative acts can always be established by comparing their consequences and weighing the benefits and harm on a quantitative scale. As we have seen, this approach to morality as such will not work, inasmuch as human values cannot be reduced to a common denominator and measured on a common scale. But where comparisons can be made, as sometimes happens (when one is confronted with different ways of realizing the same good), it is both appropriate and morally responsible to make them.

Where, morally speaking, efficiency is possible, it is a virtue, although it is no virtue if it means achieving a limited objective at the expense of violating some basic good. By contrast, waste and inefficiency are signs of vice, although it is no vice to be judged inefficient in the pursuit of an objective when efficiency would require the violation of fundamental human goods.

A nation, for instance, might be judged inefficient in defending—or failing to defend—itself against aggression, even to the point of allowing itself to be overrun and conquered. But such inefficiency would not be immoral—it would in fact reflect an entirely moral attitude—if the efficiency required to repel aggression came down in cold fact to attacking the actual or potential invader's civilian population.

As this example suggests, the modes of responsibility apply not only to individuals but also to communities in their common action. They hold, in other words, not only for persons singly but for persons collectively. Each mode of responsibility has a social dimension as well as an individual dimension.

It is worth noting, too, that various ethical or pseudoethical theories have seized upon one or several of these modes of responsibility in isolation from the rest and attempted to make it or them the sole criterion of morality. This is the case, for instance, with utilitarianism, which attempts to reduce all morality to the sixth mode of responsibility (efficiency).

Many moral theories similarly go wrong, not so much by basing themselves on false principles, as by taking too limited a view of moral principles and excluding others equally as valid as the ones acknowledged. By ignoring other principles—other modes of responsibility—they fall into the trap of exclusivity, which is ultimately fatal to moral goodness. This is not to say that thinkers who propose such theories were or are morally evil; it is only to say that their theories will not lead people to moral goodness as they were meant to do.

Goodness is not found in respecting one mode of responsibility only, any more than it is found in respecting only one basic human good. Instead, moral goodness requires recognition and observance at the same time of all the modes of responsibility which we have discussed here and of two we shall examine in the chapters that follow.

Questions for Review and Discussion

1. Would you rate the first mode of responsibility—consistent commitment to a harmonious set of purposes—relatively easy or one of the more difficult to fulfill? Why?

2. Kant, who bases his ethics on the second mode of responsibility, rejects as too narrow the formulation "Do unto others as you would have them do unto you." Instead he offers the formulation "Act so that the maxim of your action can at the same time serve as a universal law." Compare these formulations with each other and with the formulation offered in the text.

3. Can you think of striking examples in which the third mode of responsibility (willingness to help others and accept responsibility for their needs) is fulfilled? In which it is violated?

4. Detachment and fidelity (the fourth and fifth modes of responsibility) seem to go in opposite directions. The idea is to exclude fanaticism on the one hand and noninvolvement on the other. Discuss concrete cases which illustrate the difficulty—yet also the possibility—of steering a middle course between these two extremes.

5. Do you think it is likely that a detached person will sometimes seem cold and unenthusiastic and that a faithful person will sometimes seem overzealous and almost fanatical? What are the signs of real detachment and fidelity?

6. The sixth mode of responsibility—to act efficiently in order to realize specific objectives—corresponds to the utilitarian outlook. As a mode of responsibility, in our sense, how does it differ from the very principle of morality itself?

7. In this chapter we illustrate the sixth mode of responsibility with an example which applies to a society rather than to an individual. Illustrate the other five modes with examples which also apply to societies of various kinds.

8. Can you think of reasons for the tendency to build an entire ethics around one or two modes of responsibility and neglect the others?

9. Moral arguments typically move from a discussion of what is involved in a particular action and the facts of the case back to some assumed moral rules, which are then criticized by appealing to modes of responsibility. Analyze some examples of actual or fictional moral arguments which reveal this pattern.

12: Duties: Responsibilities in Community

Duty and morality are virtually synonymous in many people's minds, so that doing your duty is taken as the sum and substance of moral goodness. There is, as we have seen, a great deal more to morality than this. But it is nevertheless true that duty is an extremely important mode of responsibility as well as an extremely complex one.

Duties are essentially social. They arise in structured relationships with other people. The concept of duty, as we shall see at greater length below, applies not only to individuals but to communities; and a community can have duties with regard to individual persons and also with regard to other communities. For all that, however, there are basically only two kinds of duty.

1. Contractual Duty

One might be called contractual duty. As the name suggests, it arises on the basis of a contract or agreement. An individual wants to achieve a certain objective and needs someone else's help; in order to get the help, he or she agrees to do something for the other person in return. A very simple example: a man wants his house painted and agrees to pay the painter to do the job. In such a situation each party to the bargain has a duty to fulfill his or her part of the bargain.

There will of course be exceptions. For example, one has no responsibility for carrying out an agreement to do something that is morally wrong. A hired gunman has no real duty to kill the person he is paid to assassinate. Again, responsibility under a contract disappears when circumstances change in such a way that it would be disastrous for one of the parties to fulfill the agreement. A circus tightrope walker is not required to go up on the high wire when feeling dizzy, even in order to meet the terms of a contract with the circus management.

However, no special mode of responsibility beyond those already considered seems necessary to deal with contractual duties. In order to see why one should generally keep one's agreements—and also why one should sometimes not keep them—it is enough to consider that this is how one would want others to treat oneself (the second mode of responsibility considered in the previous chapter). Unless there is general assent that "Do unto others as you would have them do unto you" is a valid moral principle, there can be no workable contracts and agreements; otherwise it would be necessary to assume that agreements either are made only to be broken or must be made so that they cannot be broken, no matter what the change in circumstances.

Generally speaking, contracts and agreements similar to them represent the coordination of people's actions at the second level of action. The actions required under contracts are specific means to specific objectives. Contracts are immensely important—indeed, essential—in everyday life, but, morally speaking, they do not raise many special problems and they are not very interesting. Far more difficult and significant, in ethical terms, is the question of duty as it relates to social relationships involving and based upon third-level action.

2. Communities and Duties

We all have a variety of social roles arising from membership in various communities, and each of these social roles
carries with it a variety of duties. To see why these duties are
normally real *moral* responsibilities—why, that is, they concern good and evil and why they involve our self-
determination—it is necessary to bear in mind what constitutes a genuine community.

A crowd of people brought together by accident or
force—by something extrinsic to the members of the
group—is not a community. Instead, a community is constituted by a kind of third-level act in which two or more people
engage together, so that it becomes in a real way their action in
common. A community is characterized by shared commitment on its members' part to the realization of some fundamental human purpose or purposes and by structures and
activity appropriate to bringing this about.

A good family is in many respects a model of community.
Its members are joined by ties of mutual dependence, to be
sure, but also by a joint commitment to common purposes of a
very basic and intimate sort. Husband and wife are one flesh,
and the children are offspring of their parents' bodies. The
family members learn together, growing in knowledge by
conversation in which they share experiences and insights.
Similarly, they participate together in recreation and in religious acts. They serve and care for one another. They share
the same property. Each contributes to the community according to ability and receives according to need. By contrast,
where commitment to such basic goods is lacking, a particular
family may exist as a socioeconomic unit—as a convenient and
perhaps even congenial arrangement—but it is not a genuine
community as the word is understood and used here.

Definite structures and activity are required for the realization of the purposes which constitute a community. Institu-

tions are necessary to articulate the purposes to which the community members are committed. This in turn gives rise to various roles—what one might call "job descriptions"—for the different community members. Within the family, for instance, "father" refers to one role, "mother" to another, "oldest daughter" to a third, and so on. In saying this we are not engaging in stereotyping. Job descriptions within a particular community, whether it be the family or any other, can and do change, and it is proper to reexamine them periodically to insure that they are just and workable. Our point is only that within any community various roles and tasks are assigned to its members according to some more or less clear pattern.

The fulfillment of these roles will require that people act in certain ways. These required ways of acting are duties, and a duty may be defined as something one has a responsibility for doing or not doing by virtue of one's role in a particular community. Just as we have many social roles, so we have many duties: as citizens, as family members, as students, as employers or employees, and so on.

A community cannot function efficiently if its members do not live up to their roles and fulfill their duties. True as this is, however, it is not this which makes duties genuine moral responsibilities. Rather, the aspect of moral responsibility enters in because of the fact that the members of a community are engaged in a joint third-level action seeking the realization of a fundamental human purpose or purposes.

Community members who do not fulfill their roles and live up to their duties are in effect seeking to enjoy participation in the common good for which the community is organized without putting into it what is required of them if the community is to continue to realize the good for which it exists. They are trying to get something for nothing, to enjoy a free ride at the expense of other community members. Moreover, they are undermining the community at its roots by refusing to do their part to realize its purposes. If enough members behave in this way, the result, sooner or later, will be the collapse of the community and the end of the possibility that *this* community will realize its constituting purposes.

When one reflects upon the attitude of community members who neglect or refuse to carry out their duties, it is clear that they care less about the good upon which the community is grounded than about their own enjoyment of that good. They are in the community for what they can get out of it, not for what they can contribute to joint realization of the community's shared commitment. Their attitude toward other members of the community is basically exploitative: they seek to use others in order to realize their self-interest, instead of working with and for others so that all together may participate more fully in the purpose which brought them together. This exploitative attitude is fundamentally inimical to and destructive of community.

This point also can be explained in terms of the levels of action. A community is constituted by a shared commitment, which is at the third level of action. Members who do not do their duty transform their own actions from third-level participation in the common good to actions at the second level, directed now to the limited objective of getting out of the situation what can be gotten for themselves. Such people naturally hope that other members of the community will continue to fulfill their duties in a dedicated way. (It should not be supposed that this explanation means that such persons have *no* "third-level" purpose in view. They do, but it is not the common good. Rather it is some good or goods of particular interest and concern to themselves—perhaps some aspect of their own self-integration or "self-fulfillment.")

Having said this, however, it is necessary to add two important qualifications. First our duties as community members are real moral responsibilities only if the community itself is oriented to the realization of goods in a proper way—is not, in other words, a manipulative, exploitative arrangement masquerading as community but actually designed for the benefit and gratification of a few. Second, when duties conflict with one another, as they sometimes do, our moral responsibility is limited to fulfilling only one of the conflicting duties, but deciding which one is not at all easy. Both points deserve closer examination.

3. In Search of Community

A pure community with no elements of injustice and exploitation is a rare thing—so rare that it is doubtful whether such a phenomenon ever does exist in our imperfect world. Certainly the large-scale societies of which we are all members are not pure communities. They have aspects of genuine community, but they have less attractive aspects as well. And our duties as members of such a society are true moral responsibilities only when they arise from the community aspect of the society rather than from its unjust and exploitative aspects.

Nations, including the United States, are such societies: partly community and partly a highly complex structure to facilitate self-interest and exploitation. To say this is not to engage in breast-beating or viewing-with-alarm; it is simply to state the evident fact of the matter.

As a community, the United States is well over two hundred million people joined in a commitment to realize a number of noble purposes which find verbal expression in such formulations as the Preamble to the Constitution. This is the reality underlying the notion of government by the consent of the governed. It is important to note, however, that the consent envisioned here has a special meaning. It is not merely a mutual agreement among individuals that some measure of government is necessary to protect their individual security and welfare, as well as the security and welfare of those for whom they are concerned. This is part of it, but a further part of the consent in question is shared concern for goods recognized as possessing an inherent goodness which appeals to reasonable persons. The consent of the governed is consent founded in recognition of basic human goods.

While this kind of joint commitment is certainly an aspect of the nation, it is not the total picture. Side by side with it one finds ample evidence that some individuals and groups receive preferred treatment.

Loopholes in tax laws, for example, allow some segments of society to escape most taxes while other citizens find their taxes soaring; the simple fact of being born with a white skin instead of black or brown or yellow tends to insure one of privileges and prerogatives which black-, brown-, and yellow-skinned people seldom enjoy and then only with great difficulty. So to some extent does the fact of being born a man rather than a woman. And so in certain circumstances does the fact of being an adult human being in pursuit of self-interest rather than an unborn human being lacking means of either pursuing or protecting self-interest.

Quite simply, one can take it for granted that any large society will be only an approximation of a true community. At its best it will be an expression of community. At its worst it will be a system for exploitation. Between its best and its worst it will be a system of more or less fair deals and arrangements in which community can degenerate under the eroding force of exploitation.

What does all this imply for our duties as members of such societies? Simply that such duties are real moral responsibilities only to the extent that they flow from our roles in institutions which articulate the fundamental commitment of the society-as-community. On the other hand, to the extent that duties arise from some form of institutionalized exploitation they are not moral responsibilities, and in some cases one may even have the responsibility of refusing to carry out such a duty.

An example makes this clearer. Slavery is an extreme form of institutionalized exploitation, yet slavery has been accepted in many societies throughout history. Even the United States, which articulated its belief in and commitment to essential human equality at the time of its founding, simultaneously recognized the institution of slavery and sanctioned it in law.

Slaves, as members of such a society, have a duty to submit to their enslavement; and this duty will be embodied in laws which provide, among other things, for their punishment if they are bad slaves. But no one today seriously supposes that this duty carries with it any real moral responsibility. In short, in a society which accepts slavery as a social institution some people may have a social duty to be slaves, but they can have no moral responsibility arising from this role, and it is not immoral of them to refuse their duty. (Of course, this does not mean that a slave has no moral responsibilities at all. At times a slave might be required by one of the other modes of responsibility to endure with patience even the injustice of the condition of slavery.)

Slavery is a case in which societies have given institutional expression of a rather extreme variety to exploitation, and the consequent social duties are not moral responsibilities. But there are also other cases in which social duty does not carry any moral responsibility. It sometimes happens, for example, that the purposes of a society which one joined voluntarily change. In such a case one has a moral responsibility only in regard to duties which reflect the purposes of the society at the time one accepted membership; one has no responsibility to fulfill duties which reflect new purposes to which one does not subscribe.

If, for instance, one joins a recreational club, and the club later begins to change its orientation to some form of political activism, the mere fact that one is a member of the club does not impose any moral responsibility to join in its political activities if one has not subscribed to this new orientation.

Something similar happens when changing circumstances

bring about a change in the fairness of the division of labor within a society. Perhaps over a period of time the amount of effort required in one area diminishes while that involved in another area increases greatly, so that after a while some members of the group find themselves doing very little work and others doing a great deal. In such a case, something like exploitation has crept into the society without anyone's really intending it. When this happens it is time for the society to take a fresh look at the situation and redivide the duties. And if the beneficiaries of the imbalance refuse to do so, as sometimes happens, the victims have no moral responsibility to continue to carry out their duties.

Even this abbreviated discussion makes it apparent that this is a very complicated subject. While it is easy enough to say in the abstract that duties which arise from bad laws and other exploitative social institutions are not moral responsibilities, in reality it may be irresponsible not to tolerate a certain amount of injustice in society. The tax laws, for instance, may not be altogether just, but if all citizens stopped paying their taxes for this reason or felt free to cheat on their tax returns, the result would more likely be chaos than reform. Achieving and constantly maintaining perfect balance and perfect justice in the ever-changing conditions of a society are simply not possible.

Knowing when to comply with duties that lack the force of moral responsibilities and when to refuse to comply often requires a subtle discernment which cannot be programmed in advance. To refer again to the example of taxes, it may in practice be quite difficult to balance one's recognition of the general obligation to pay one's fair share against one's moral repugnance at paying to help support policies and practices which are clearly immoral. At least, though, it should be clear that not every social duty is also a moral responsibility and that people may at times have a right to refuse to carry out some duties. In fact, if carrying out a particular duty would be immoral on other grounds, one's moral responsibility is to refuse to carry it out. This is the principle of conscientious objection.

4. When Duties Conflict

Equally complicated is the situation of an individual whose duties as a member of different communities come into conflict with one another. A businessman is scheduled to make an important out-of-town trip for his company; the day before he is to leave, his wife comes down with a bad case of the flu. If he does not make the trip, a deal on which the company has been counting is likely to fall through; if he does make the trip, his wife will have to go on taking care of the children and the house when she ought properly to be in bed. What should he do—go or stay?

There is no a priori answer to that question. Taken individually, each duty would be a moral responsibility. But the duties are now in head-on conflict. The answer will be different for different individuals; the most we can do here is point to certain guidelines which are applicable to any such case.

For one thing, if it is not really impossible to fulfill both duties, one has a moral responsibility to do so; but if it is really impossible, one does not have a moral responsibility to do so. We are never morally responsible for doing the impossible. Furthermore, since either of the conflicting duties would be a moral responsibility if it were not for the other, one has a definite moral responsibility to fulfill one or the other of the duties. The businessman-husband of our example is morally obliged either to make the trip or to stay home with his wife; he may not cop out by refusing to do either. Further still, there are no general principles by which to say that the weight of moral responsibility lies in the direction of one duty or the other. Since both are serious duties, the individual will be doing the morally right thing if he does either—provided, of course, that he does it in the right way and for the right reasons.

But what are the right way and the right reasons? To begin with, people in conflict situations should be honest in making their choices. If an individual in such a situation considers how he or she would feel in the position of each of the others involved, and *then* opts in a way he or she would really consider unreasonable from the viewpoint of one of the other positions, this may well be a violation of another mode of responsibility, the second one. As a matter of fact, the second mode underlies the seventh, and in conflict of duty situations one has to fall back on it: Do unto others as you would have them do unto you.

It is reasonable, furthermore, to doubt an individual's honesty if, whenever conflicts arise, he or she always opts for one set of duties and against the other. In the example given, it may be that the businessman consistently puts his job before his family. If so, and if in this situation, too, he chooses the job-related duty over the family-related one, it is likely that his choice is really an expression of a selfish bias rather than an honest judgment of moral responsibility.

In addition, people faced with conflicting duties should take practical steps to try to resolve their quandary. Perhaps, if he tried, the businessman could postpone his trip after all; or perhaps he could make arrangements for a relative or friend to care for his wife and the children while he is out of town.

People in such situations should also try to discuss their problem with the other party or parties involved in order to obtain their suggestions and to determine as far as possible who will be most hurt by the nonfulfillment of duty. Perhaps the businessman will discover that his colleagues do not consider the trip as important as he does or that his wife is not really so very sick and does not object to his leaving.

The fact that duties can and sometimes do conflict underlines the need for exercising great care in making commitments and accepting membership in different communities. It is rash to take on a variety of social roles carrying duties which one might with forethought have known would come into conflict. In practice, this means that people should attempt to organize their lives so that as far as possible their various roles and duties complement and support one another instead of conflicting.

It reflects not only good planning but a morally correct attitude when a person's family life, career, civic and church responsibilities, and other social roles mesh in a harmonious and consistent manner. To be sure, no one can be so farsighted as to eliminate conflicts of duty entirely from his or her life, and in our society it is more difficult for some people than for others: for example, more difficult for some women who must try to combine work outside the home with maternal responsibilities than for many men. Nevertheless it is not only sensible but a moral responsibility to try to prevent conflicts as much as possible and, when conflicts do inevitably arise, to act with a combination of honesty and practicality in attempting to resolve them.

Up to now we have considered seven of the modes of responsibility. The eighth is yet to come. It is the subject of the next chapter.

Questions for Review and Discussion

1. If moral responsibility is limited to duty, what sort of theory is likely to result?

2. If duties were the only mode of responsibility, would cultural relativism (or relativity of morals to each society) be true?

3. Contractual duties are fairly obvious forms of responsibility, and sometimes the effort is made to ground all duties in a "social contract." What do such attempts imply concerning the theory of the individual and society?

4. It has been suggested that even the duties which arise from genuine community can be reduced to other modes of responsibility, such as the second and the fifth, so that no separate, seventh mode of responsibility is needed. Discuss this point of view.

5. Our section entitled "In search of community" suggests, but does not spell out, a theory of social justice. Can you articulate this theory more clearly? Compare it with classic theories such as the following: (1) that each individual should receive from the society according to merit (Aristotle); (2) that each should contribute according to ability and receive according to need (Marx); and (3) that each should promote as far as possible the equality of all members (liberal democracy).

6. Some ethical theories suppose there can be a conflict of moral responsibilities. How does our position on conflict of duties differ?

7. In case of conflict of duties, how might it help to invoke other modes of responsibility, such as the second?

8. Think of actual or fictional examples of conflict of duties and discuss the manner in which they were resolved.

9. Sartre suggests as typical of the situation of moral choice a case in which a young man during World War II must decide either to stay with his aged mother who needs his care or join his friends in the French underground. He points out that the young man's commitment alone will determine which is right and from this concludes that moral responsibility is subjective. Criticize this line of argument in light of what we have learned about duties.

13: Persons, Means, and Ends

Are there ethical absolutes? Are there principles which should never be violated and therefore things which should never be done, regardless of the circumstances and the consequences?

Almost instinctively most people would answer Yes, and then would go on to cite some action which they feel should never be performed: purposely to torture a small child, for instance. Yet for many ethical theorists the answer is No. For them there are no ethical absolutes and therefore no actions which can flatly be ruled out as beyond the pale of acceptable human behavior.

This is not to suggest that such theorists are themselves vicious or immoral. People who do not believe in ethical absolutes may indeed be high-minded and right-living—in particular cases more so perhaps than those who hold that there are some actions which ought never to be performed.

The issue here, however, is not whose private life and personal conduct are more upstanding and blameless. The question is, rather, Whose ethical position is true? Is any action whatsoever allowable, at least in certain circumstances? Or are there actions which it is never morally right to perform?

The eighth mode of responsibility states unequivocally that there are such actions. It may be put quite simply: It is never right to act directly against one of the fundamental human

135

goods. "To act directly against a good" means to make a choice to destroy, damage, or impede that good in one or more instances. But easy as it is to state this principle, it is more difficult to show what it means. The question is far removed from idle speculation, however. Indeed, it is one of the most burning ethical issues of our times, an issue with far-reaching practical ramifications for individual and social life.

1. Duties and Responsibilities

In our discussion of duties we saw that many moral responsibilities arise from duties (which in turn arise from our structured social relationships with other people). Such responsibilities have true moral force, but they are not absolute. This is evident from the fact that they can and sometimes do conflict with one another. A man's responsibilities arising from his duties as a husband and father may sometimes come into conflict with his responsibilities as an employee. Both sets of duties are real, but in a particular situation an individual may not be able to respond to both.

People in such situations must fulfill one set of duties and neglect the other. Provided they are honest about the facts and their response to the facts, they can do so with a clear conscience, in the knowledge that these duties, while real, are not absolute responsibilities and, where circumstances require, can be neglected in favor of other, equally pressing duties.

However, there are other responsibilities which do not arise from duties and which are not conditional but absolute. They are founded on the implications of the ideal of openness to all the goods constitutive of the human person.

Openness to the human goods or purposes is the basis of a right moral attitude. In acting directly against any one of them either we carry out destructive emotional urges or we make that against which we act a means to an ulterior end. But the goods that go to make up personhood are themselves the ends of human action, and as such they should not be treated as if they were objects on which to vent our feelings or mere means to other ends. Because each of these goods is, as we have seen, the supreme good in its own way, no one of them may be treated with contempt or subordinated to another as a means to an end. Thus the minimum requirement for a morally correct attitude (and action) is simultaneous respect for all the basic goods: respect which in practice means refusing to violate any fundamental good either out of impulse or in order to achieve some further good.

The seven modes of responsibility which we have examined up to now are positive: they tell us what to do. This eighth mode is negative. It tells us what we ought *not* to do. It is not correct to suppose that all morality is summed up in prohibition ("thou shalt not"), although it is sometimes caricatured in that way. But it is also a mistake to overlook the extremely strong binding force of this negative mode of responsibility: One should never act directly against any one of the fundamental human goods.

Everyone at times becomes angry; everyone at times feels hatred toward others and even toward himself or herself. Destructive feelings are not in a person's direct control. But we do have a responsibility for controlling such impulses in indirect ways and for restraining ourselves from harming ourselves or others to satisfy negative feelings. No matter how difficult it is to fulfill perfectly this responsibility in practice, no decent person doubts that this is a very real and serious responsibility. Moreover this responsibility is not at all difficult to understand. Hence we say no more about it here and turn our attention in the remainder of the chapter to what is more complex: the responsibility not to violate any fundamental good for the sake of an ulterior end.

What does this notion of acting directly against one of the fundamental goods in order to achieve some further good really entail? In practice something like the following. A person who is about to choose in a morally wrong way is about to adopt a proposal which involves detriment or injury to a human good. He or she is inclined to accept this detriment to one good because it contributes to the realization of another good. Clearly, such an individual either has already made or is about to make a determination that the good which will be realized outweighs the good which will suffer injury. Yet as a matter of fact the two goods are incommensurable: neither outweighs the other; both are basic elements of human personhood. In adopting such a proposal, nevertheless, an individual simply cannot remain open to the good which will suffer detriment, for this good is going to be violated. In adopting the proposal he or she also necessarily accepts this violation and in doing so adopts, at least implicitly, a narrowed and restricted view of the purposes which go to make up human personhood: that is, of personhood itself.

It is essential to bear in mind that these goods or purposes are what human life and action are all about. The language we use here is unavoidably abstract. But the goods themselves are not abstractions, existing "out there" beyond us and other people. Rather, as we experience them, they are aspects of human beings, ourselves or others—aspects which either already exist in actuality or have the potential of being realized. To act directly against one of the fundamental goods is therefore to violate an actual or possible aspect of the personhood of a real person or persons: to violate "life," for example, means violating *somebody's* life. This amounts to using a human person as a means to an end.

2. Are There Inalienable Rights?

Critics of the view that there are ethical absolutes sometimes refer to them disparagingly as "legalistic absolutes." Rhetoric aside, the implication is that this position exalts law (legalism) at the expense of the person. But the defense of ethical absolutes, properly understood, does not mean assigning primacy to bloodless law over flesh and blood persons. On the contrary, it constitutes a defense of persons and their inalienable rights.

If there are no absolute responsibilities, there are no inalienable rights. If it were true that any action, no matter what it might be, is permitted in certain circumstances, then no good intrinsic to the person would be safe from invasion and suppression, provided the justifying circumstances existed. This is true even in regard to ethical theories which propose the existence of virtual absolutes: norms which proponents of such theories say they can hardly conceive in practice as being subject to violation and actions whose justifying circumstances they can scarcely envision as ever arising. While the proponents of such theories may not be able to envision such circumstances, others less idealistic are quite able to imagine— and find—just the circumstances in which people can be sacrificed to the attainment of ulterior ends.

If there are no ethical absolutes, human persons, rather than being the norm and source from which other things receive their value, become simply items or commodities with a relative value—inviolable only up to the point at which it is expedient to violate them in order to achieve an objective. It would then make no sense at all to speak of the immeasurable value of the human person. Far from being immeasurable— that is, beyond calculation—the value of a person would be quite specific and quantifiable, something to be weighed in the balance against other values.

As a matter of fact, it is often assumed that just this sort of weighing of human goods and human persons is possible. The assumption enters in, tacitly in many instances, as a result of confusion between the fundamental goods constitutive of the person, which are always open-ended and never fully defined (because one can never say that one of these goods has been totally realized and exhausted by oneself or others) and a specific objective which is never completely identical with the person.

Typically, an individual with such an attitude will think along the following lines: Two lives are better than one; therefore if two innocent lives can be saved by sacrificing one innocent life, it is entirely right and proper to sacrifice the one life in order to save the two.

An example dramatizes this attitude. In wartime a military commander is confronted with a group of prisoners who possess important information about the enemy's plans. He needs the information in order to prevent loss of life among his own troops, but the prisoners will not tell him what he wants to know. In order to compel the prisoners to talk, he has one of them executed as an example to the others and thereby frightens the survivors into divulging the desired information. By taking one life he has saved other lives, and according to the principle that two lives are better than one (or twenty better than two, or two thousand better than twenty, and so on) his action seems not only expedient but morally right.

One arrives at a very different judgment, however, if human life is regarded, not as a concrete, specific, essentially quantifiable object, but as a good in which each person participates but which none exhausts or sums up alone. In denying the theory that two lives are better than one we really are denying that two persons are worth twice as much as some other real person. On this view it is simply not possible to make the sort of calculation which weighs lives against each other (my life is more valuable than John's life, John's life is more valuable than Mary's and Tom's combined, or vice versa) and thus to determine whose life shall be respected and whose sacrificed. The value of life, each human life, is incalculable, not in any merely poetic sense, but simply because it is something not susceptible to calculation, measurement, weighing, and balancing.

Traditionally this point has been expressed by the statement that the end does not justify the means. This is a way of saying that the direct violation of any good intrinsic to the person cannot be justified by the good result which such a violation will bring about. What is extrinsic to human persons may be used for the good of persons, but what is intrinsic to persons has a kind of sacredness and may not be violated.

Returning to our earlier analysis of human action, it should be apparent that the attitude which regards goods intrinsic to the person as inviolable is inclusivistic: one remains open to all the goods even though one cannot always act to realize each of them. On the other hand, the attitude that any basic good of persons can directly be violated if circumstances require this in order to achieve another good is exclusivistic: the good not chosen becomes, by that fact, worthless—so worthless, indeed, that one can act directly to its detriment. Using persons as means to an end is always wrong. It betrays the fact that one does not love the whole constellation of human goods in an inclusivistic way, but rather loves this part as against that part: loves the part one chooses or furthers in preference to the part which one uses as one's means. And since these goods are not apart from persons, a selective love of goods is a selective love of persons.

3. Ethical Absolutes and Utilitarian Solutions

Ultimately, of course, the conviction that there are no ethical absolutes and that, in consequence, there is no action

no ethical absolutes

which could not in some circumstances, however remote, be morally justifiable represents a utilitarian approach to the question of ethics and action. In concluding this chapter it may be worth speculating on why this attitude has become so common in our times and society and, in particular, why it is so evident in regard to the fundamental human good of life.

No one reflecting upon the events of the twentieth century can fail to be struck by the fact that something frightening has entered the picture in regard to attitudes toward human life (not the quality of life, but life itself). No doubt on some issues ethical sensitivity has moved forward in our times, but one can hardly make this judgment with regard to respect for life. The massacre of millions of human beings in Hitler's Germany, Stalin's Russia, the Khmer Rouge's Cambodia, and other countries is terrible evidence of the fact that at the very least the twentieth century has been no more respectful of life than were past centuries—has, if anything, become more casual, as well as more efficient, about the taking of life.

What of our own society? The picture is not appreciably brighter here. It was the United States, after all, which dropped the first atomic bombs—on Hiroshima and Nagasaki—justifying this action by the argument that it would save lives. The alternative of accepting Japan's surrender on reasonable terms was not seriously considered until after the atomic bombs were dropped.

One might be tempted to dismiss the atomic bombing of these two cities as an isolated aberration, an action performed in the heat of wartime passion and later regretted. But it is not really possible to accept this explanation. The fact is that since that time the United States has put the world on notice that if circumstances were to require, it would do to other cities and their civilian populations even worse than it did to Hiroshima and Nagasaki. That, after all, is a central element of the American nuclear deterrent strategy: a strategy which affirms that if pressed to the wall in war, the United States would rain down nuclear bombs on enemy cities. Leaving aside the question of whether such a course of action would in any sense be rational (although it would in fact be the height of irrationality), the strategy is built on the presumption that the United States would really do what it says it is prepared to do. Otherwise the deterrent would not be credible.

Our intention is not to enter into the intricacies of international politics and defense strategy. The point is simply that if the United States did what it says it is prepared to do (and the presumption of the American government and people must be that it is in deadly earnest about this), it would have performed an act of unparalleled immorality. In that case it is terrible to contemplate the judgment of future generations, if any.

For years, though, we have been living with the knowledge and intention that this is how the United States would, in certain circumstances, act. And it is submitted that, in subtle but real ways, this fact—of the nuclear deterrent strategy and all it implies—has undermined the foundations of moral perception and moral thought in our society. This is a broad statement, and one whose truth it is impossible to demonstrate in the confines of this parenthetical speculation. Yet it stands to reason that this appalling fact has, like a sort of moral disease, infected national life, deadened ethical sensitivity, and poisoned many aspects of our society.

We do not propose a solution. We only suggest that the nuclear deterrent strategy represents a frighteningly logical application of the principle that the end *does* justify the means. And, having willingly although regretfully accepted this principle in one critical area of national life, we can hardly expect to be immune from its influence in many others.

Finally, it is necessary to acknowledge that acceptance of the principle that there are ethical absolutes—that the end does not justify the means—implies willingness to accept or tolerate some finite damage rather than act directly against one of the fundamental human goods. A nation unwilling to act unjustly in war, for example, may have to accept defeat; an individual unwilling to act dishonestly in a competitive situation may have to accept some financial or other loss.

Those who assert the position that the end does justify the means will frequently assert as well that this readiness to suffer damage is unreasonable. But to one who is determined not to limit the meaning of human life to the quantifiable, who is determined instead to preserve the inviolability of the person against threats and infringements, it will be the most reasonable thing in the world.

We have now considered all eight modes of responsibility. They do indeed give us moral guidelines; yet we are obliged to recognize that applying them is by no means a cut-and-dried matter. Doing so can in fact be excruciatingly difficult in the case of action which is or seems to be ambiguous. In the next chapter we shall examine this problem and see how it can be resolved.

Questions for Review and Discussion

1. What characteristic distinguishes the eighth mode of responsibility from the first seven?

2. Some who reject moral absolutes argue against them as legalism and say law is made for human beings, not human beings for the law. How can this challenge be answered within the framework of the present approach to ethics?

3. The eighth mode of responsibility leads to negative moral rules. Does the negative form of such rules point to a theoretical priority of evil over good?

4. There is a sense in which good ends do justify the means necessary to achieve them, provided these means are not in some way morally objectionable in themselves. With this in mind, clarify the saying "The end doesn't justify the means."

5. We mention in this chapter some military-political examples of

the doctrine that the end does justify the means. Think of examples involving each of the categories of fundamental human purposes in which someone might be tempted to go directly against the good for the sake of an ulterior purpose.

6. One who holds the utilitarian point of view often will argue against the eighth mode of responsibility by proposing examples in which there seems to be a huge disproportion between the damage done if one refuses to act directly against one of the goods which constitutes the person and the damage if one does so act. Can you suggest a strategy to be used in dealing with such examples?

7. There was an ancient Stoic maxim "Let right be done, though the heavens fall." Is this a fair statement of the philosophy involved in the eighth mode of responsibility?

8. To what extent do you think it might be possible to accept the rest of the ethical theory outlined in this book while rejecting the eighth mode of responsibility? In other words, how much can be salvaged by someone who likes the approach in general but is unable to agree with this last mode of responsibility?

14: When Action Is Ambiguous

Seldom is life as simple as one might wish. In ethics this truism is amply illustrated by the problems posed by actions which have more than one aspect. Looked at in one way, such an action seems to promote the realization of a human good and therefore to be itself ethically good. Looked at another way, it is seen to be detrimental to a human good and therefore appears ethically evil.

How evaluate an action with such intrinsic ambiguity? Does one properly emphasize the positive and, concentrating on the good aspect, judge the act to be morally good? Or is it ethically correct to place the emphasis on the evil aspect and judge the act morally wrong? As a practical matter, may one or may one not perform such an action?

This is not a decision to be made casually on the basis of a hasty judgment. Confronted with an apparent dilemma of this sort, one must look closely at the action in question in order to determine what is really going on. Only on the basis of a clear-sighted analysis of the action is it possible to determine whether it is right or wrong to perform it.

1. Not Either/Or but Both/And

At this point it is important to recall something said earlier: Morality is not a matter only of external behavior, nor is it a

146

matter only of internal intention. Both are important, and the
two things are inseparable in human action. To determine the
morality of an action, one must always answer two questions:
"What am I doing? Why am I doing it?" It is not enough to
answer only one of these questions.

This point is important here because of the temptation
some may feel to solve the problem of ambiguous action by
saying that a good intention is sufficient to make such an
action morally good. This is the position taken, for example,
by those who attempt to resolve what they sometimes call the
"agonizing dilemma" involved in the abortion decision by referring exclusively to the intentions of the individual or individuals involved. Thus: "It is certainly repugnant to me that
the unborn child should die, but that is not really my intention. I am only interested in sparing this woman avoidable
pain and suffering."

It is, however, not really that easy. As far as morality is
concerned, the what and why of action are inseparable. In the
case of abortion the *what* is the killing of an unborn human
life; it is not possible for any *why*—that is, a good intention—
to change this. (It should be noted, too, that reducing
morality to a matter of good intentions alone opens the door
dangerously wide to rationalizations of all sorts. If they try
hard enough, people can always find good intentions for what
they propose to do, so that if good intentions were all that
mattered, it would be possible to justify doing almost anything.)

If, then, one cannot solve the problem of ambiguous action
simply by relying on good intentions, it is necessary to find
another approach. The key lies in closely examining the action involved to determine its real structure. If it is an indivisible unity and if it directly realizes a human good, persons
performing the act for the sake of the good in which it allows
them or others to participate need not be wrongly disposed
toward the good which is simultaneously damaged; and pro-

vided they are not so disposed, their action might possibly be morally upright.

If, on the other hand, their intention does include detriment to the good which is damaged, then they are acting wrongly in performing the act. If, furthermore, analysis of the action reveals that its two aspects are in fact related to each other as means and end (the good result is only attained in an act distinct from that in which the bad is caused), then one must invoke the principle that the end does not justify the means and conclude that it is immoral to perform the action.

These sentences are packed with meaning and deal with complex matters. For the rest of this chapter we shall be attempting to explain what they say and why they say it.

2. Two Kinds of Ambiguity

As has just been suggested, the ambiguity of ambiguous action can be of two kinds. In one type the destructive aspect of the action is the means by which the positive aspect is realized. In the second the two aspects are really inseparably linked in the one action: the positive aspect does not produce the destructive, nor does the destructive produce the positive; one act encompasses both results directly.

An example will help make this clearer. There was a time when boys with beautiful soprano voices were castrated so that their voices would not change and they could continue to sing in a choir. The action had two aspects: it was a mutilation of the body, an attack upon an aspect of the basic good of life; it was also a *means* to facilitate the beautiful music which was desired to give glory to God. Clearly, however, the mutilation was one action and the production of the music a quite distinct action. Thus the two meanings of the initial act were not intrinsic to it; rather, an intrinsically mutilating act was only an extrinsic means to an end ultimately desired: namely, the beauty of the church service.

What was involved in this way of acting was that one fundamental human good (bodily integrity, which is part of the good of life itself) was subordinated to others (aesthetic and religious). But it is immoral to subordinate basic goods to each other in such a way, since all of these goods are aspects of the human person, and each of them is good in its own special and irreplaceable way. Thus, the castration of the choir boys was not morally justifiable. And this is so even though the interest of those who did this was presumably focused not on the destructive aspect of the action but on its positive effect.

Regardless of one's interest the structure of action is what it is. It does not change simply because one's primary concern is directed toward one aspect rather than another. Even though, in emotional terms, a person may not feel that he or she wants the destructive aspect of an action, it is nevertheless inescapable that it *be* intended inasmuch as it is required as the means to reach the good end toward which his or her feelings are directed.

Let us suppose, however, that a young boy is found to have a cancerous growth involving his testicles. Stopping the disease requires that the boy be castrated. Here the act also has two aspects, but it is ambiguous in a different way from the previous example. On the one hand, the integrity of the body is damaged; part of the reality of a human life is literally cut off. But, on the other hand, in the very same act the life of the person is protected so far as possible from the destructive attack of the disease.

In this case one fundamental good—or aspect of a good— is not being sacrificed for another: the relationship between the two aspects is not that of means and end. Although the damage done by the operation is foreseen and fully understood, there is a real sense in which it is inseparable from the

good to which this very act makes its own immediate contribution. The operation is not castration done as a means to an
ulterior end, but cancer-removing surgery which makes an
immediate contribution to the good of life and which incidentally and unfortunately also is permanently mutilating. The
operation is morally justifiable.

It is necessary now to relate this analysis of the structure of
ambiguous action to the person performing such action.

People are responsible primarily for their choices. What
people do is, properly speaking, that which carries out the
proposals which they adopt in making choices. Thus, what
people do constitutes them in a real sense: it directly shapes
their character. Secondarily, however, people are responsible
for the effects which come about as a result of their actions.
The effects are results of actions but not strictly part of them.

If the effects are foreseen, they are voluntary: they are
accepted by the person performing the action which produces
the effects. But there is a significant difference between the
voluntarily accepted effects of one's action and the chosen
means to one's end. The means to ends are included in the
proposals one adopts: one identifies with them. And a means
which is incompatible with or detrimental to a basic human
good cannot be adopted by an individual who understands
what he or she is doing without involving that person in immorality.

By contrast, effects which are only accepted, not intended
by the person performing the action, are, from the viewpoint
of the intention of the individual, neither compatible nor incompatible with the basic human goods. They are in themselves neither an expression of the individual's intent to
realize a good nor an expression of his or her intent to act to
the detriment of the good. Thus we see how, hypothetically at
least, an action which produces effects harmful to a good can
be performed by an individual without involving him or her

in immorality. It is possible for a person to perform such an action without violating the eighth mode of responsibility.

It is important, however, to see this matter in its full complexity. The anticipated but unintended effects of one's behavior do have an impact—an extremely important one—on fundamental human goods. Thus, although it may be possible in some cases to perform actions which are detrimental to a human good without violating the eighth mode of responsibility, one must bear in mind the possibility that in doing so one may be acting in violation of some other mode of responsibility.

If, for example, one is truly concerned for all of the goods which make up the human person, one will not show partiality or favoritism to some people at the expense of others in performing actions which have harmful (as well as beneficial) effects. Nor will one tolerate effects which one has a duty to avoid according to some other mode of responsibility. As we shall see below, it is possible that a person killing in self-defense might not violate the eighth mode of responsibility; but if such a person is a Christian who believes that Christ's message enjoins nonviolence in the face of violent aggression, such an individual will, in killing in self-defense, be acting against what he or she understands to be his or her duty as a Christian. We are not responsible for the effects we accept in exactly the same way we are responsible for our actions, but our responsibility for the effects can nevertheless be just as serious as our responsibility for the actions.

At the same time it is perfectly true that we can be so confused, in our thinking or our feelings, that we are not fully aware of the real structure of our actions. Under pressure we can confuse the two kinds of ambiguous action and so imagine that we can justify our action without adopting the maxim that the end justifies the means—while, as a matter of fact, only that maxim would rationalize what we do.

In particular cases such confusion can reduce or even entirely remove personal guilt for wrong acts. Yet a person who wants to act—or at least to judge—morally, and therefore rationally, will strive to overcome emotional and intellectual confusion so as to analyze ambiguous actions carefully and make correct moral judgments about them.

3. Killing the Unborn

Many other cases illustrate the difference between the two kinds of ambiguous action. There is, for example, an important distinction to be made concerning operations performed on pregnant women which result in death to the unborn: some kill the unborn individual as a means to an ulterior end; other actions directly result in a benefit to the mother's health and only incidentally kill the unborn.

Since abortion is such a pressing and controversial issue, it is worth remarking that it does not really matter whether or not one wishes to call the fetus a person. It is alive; it is human; it is an individual. No one can prove that it is not a person, and it needs only to be let alone for a while in order to prove to everyone that it is. Moreover, quite apart from whether one does or doesn't call the fetus a person, willingness to destroy the unborn is willingness to destroy human life. No one would deny that this is personal life except that there is pressure to kill it. And people always find subtle grounds for questioning the personhood of those whom they wish to destroy. It happened before in this country with blacks and native Americans; it is happening now with the unborn.

If a woman does not want a baby because it would interfere with her career or stretch the family budget too far or cause her embarrassment or for any other reason at all, and if she has an operation or does anything else to get rid of the unwanted pregnancy, then this is killing as a means to an end. Such action goes directly against the fundamental good of human life and is morally wrong for that reason.

Still, there are cases in which it can be permissible to perform a procedure which results in the death of the unborn child, even when this outcome is known in advance. For instance, it may be necessary to remove a cancerous womb from a pregnant woman before her unborn child is old enough to survive outside the womb. But this operation is not properly called abortion, nor need it be regarded as morally wrong. Here the death of the unborn is not the *means* of benefiting the mother. This death is only an unavoidable *side effect*, incidental to the lifesaving operation.

The structure of this action, unlike the act of abortion, does not require that one intend the death of the child, and so there is no turning against life, even though destruction of life inevitably occurs. (If, of course, those involved in such a procedure really do intend the death of the unborn child, as well as the saving of the mother's life, then the situation is radically different from the point of view of ethics, and the action is morally wrong.)

4. Other Examples

A man is walking down a dark street at night when a deranged-looking individual leaps out of the bushes, knife in hand, and attacks him. May he use force to resist such an attack? May he even kill the attacker? The answer: It depends.

According to the principle we have been examining the man is certainly justified in acting to preserve his life; in the situation described this is the good which he has preeminently in view. Since that is so, he can take action to preserve life which also results in some harm to his attacker, provided there is no alternative open to him.

But is another course of action besides the use of force
feasible? If such a practical course of action (for example,
flight or evasion instead of force) does exist, then the ethically
correct thing to do is that which will not involve harm to
another good (in this instance, injury to the attacker).

Supposing, though, that the only thing possible in the circumstances is to resist force with force, then the man should
choose a form of resistance which involves no more force than
is really necessary. Suppose the individual who has been at-
tacked is a policeman. He should, if possible, stun his attacker
with his billy club instead of shooting him with his revolver; if
it is necessary for him to use the revolver, he should shoot to
wound his assailant, not kill; he should kill only if there is
really nothing else to do.

Granted the artificiality of the example (few people,
policemen or not, would be in a position in such circumstances to make the nice determinations and judgments just
outlined), we are using it here to clarify a principle, not to
describe the mental processes of an actual person in an actual
situation. And the principle is this: If it is possible to realize
the good one has in view without engaging in an ambiguous
action which involves simultaneous harm to another good,
one should do so; if such an ambiguous action is truly unavoidable, one should act in a way that involves no avoidable
detriment to the good.

It may be objected that in this case the good which suffers
detriment is actually subordinated to the other good which is
realized as a means to an end: the policeman clubs or shoots
his assailant precisely in order to preserve his own life. Again,
we can only say: It all depends. If this is the way the policeman regards his action, then, ethically speaking, that certainly
is the way it is for him. But it is not necessary for him to
analyze his action in this manner. He can correctly view injury
to his assailant simply as the unavoidable consequence of the

behavior required on his part to repel force and protect his life. Precisely how he regards the situation and his response to it is a question which only he—and perhaps not even he—can answer with certainty.

This, however, is not the same as saying that the morality of the action is determined by how the individual happens to regard it, as if one could make an intrinsically wrong act right simply by choosing to think of it as right. The point, rather, is that the structure of the action just described is such that it can legitimately and without doing violence to reality be seen as an act whose destructive aspect is not really a means to another good but rather an unavoidable consequence of the same act in which another good is realized.

The situation is quite different, however, in a not dissimilar case: capital punishment. Leaving aside rather nebulous and unconvincing arguments for capital punishment (e.g., the assertion that in cases where a life has been taken, another life must be destroyed in order to serve the imperatives of justice—which really comes down to little more than the morality of "an eye for an eye and a tooth for a tooth"), it seems clear that the only compelling consideration in favor of capital punishment is that it serves as a deterrent to would-be criminals.

There is some evidence that capital punishment actually does not deter crime. But supposing that the deterrent argument is factually valid, it still fails to constitute an ethical justification for capital punishment. Analysis of the action of capital punishment can only lead to the conclusion that a life is being taken precisely as a means to a remote good end: the deterrence of crime. (The same thing would apply to the argument that a particular person must be executed in order to prevent *him* from committing additional crimes in the future.) Since this is so, one must conclude that there is no ethical justification for capital punishment.

5. War

Finally, it may be helpful to apply what has been said to the difficult and controversial question of warfare—not in order to pronounce on the morality of any particular war but in order to illustrate the process by which an individual might make a judgment regarding participation in war.

A great many requirements must be met before it is possible even to conclude that a military action has the quality of ambiguity discussed here. First, a military action cannot be morally acceptable if it is itself a carrying out of an unjust policy or intention. Second, it cannot be justified if there are alternative ways, short of war, for protecting or realizing the goods which are at stake. Third, there must be solid reasons for believing that the military act has a chance of being effective, of realizing the goods at which it is directed; useless killing is always immoral. Fourth, inasmuch as war is a social act, it cannot be undertaken merely on the whim or private decision of any person—even the highest public officials—but only in accord with the procedure authorized in a given society.

Still, assuming that these conditions are satisfactorily met (a very large assumption, since they seldom are), there remains the question of how an individual soldier on the battlefield should behave and how he is to judge his action. May he or may he not kill an enemy soldier?

He can look on this action—the act of killing a member of the opposing military force in time of war—in either of two ways. He can see it as killing another human being as a means to an end: saving his own life, promoting the cause for which he is fighting, or whatever; or he can see it as an action which reduces by a certain amount the unjustly used force of the opposing side.

In the latter case he is not killing for the sake of killing nor even killing for the sake of some other, presumably good end. Rather, he is performing an action directed to resisting and reducing unjust force, an action which unavoidably results in the injury or death of another person. His intention does not include detriment to the fundamental good of life, even though this good suffers detriment as one consequence of his action. As in the case of the policeman outlined above, it is not suggested that the soldier's feelings will necessarily correspond with this analysis of action. The issue, however, is not his feelings but the fundamental attitude according to which he views and engages in the act.

It should be emphasized that we are not making a defense of war. First, as we have said, the conditions which might justify a particular war are rarely satisfied in fact. Second, the requirements for an individual's participation in war—even assuming the war is not unjust as a whole—are not easily satisfied and are in fact generally ignored. But it is at least possible for an individual serving on the just side in a just war to carry out certain military duties in a morally right manner.

It is clear by now why the problem of ambiguous action is, from an ethical point of view, such a difficult one. Many different factors enter into the question: behavior, intention, close analysis of the total action in order to grasp its true structure. In real-life situations moral evaluation of such an action can be difficult, even painful. But the task is one which no one concerned with judging and living in a morally responsible manner can avoid. Furthermore, it is relevant and important even in regard to emergency situations—those in which one clearly has no time for such a process of reflection and analysis. Many of the problems which arise in emergency situations can be anticipated, at least in a general way, and in some cases are even recurrent; hence, moral analysis of ambiguous action with reference to the kinds of problems that may arise in such situations is an important preparation for the actual facing of the problems when they arise.

Up to this point we have been elaborating an approach to ethics which does indeed make it possible to answer the question of whether an action is morally good or bad. But having an approach to ethics is hardly the same thing as incorporating that approach into one's own life or helping others incorporate it into theirs. In the chapters which follow we shall consider ways in which this can be done.

Questions for Review and Discussion

1. Does the discussion in the present chapter amount to a limitation or restriction on the eighth mode of responsibility?

2. Some people think the argument presented here gives up too much—that it leads in fact to a position indistinguishable from utilitarianism. What is your opinion?

3. What difference does it make whether the good and bad aspects do or don't belong to one and the same indivisible action?

4. Can you think of examples of ambiguous acts which escape being wrong under the eighth mode of responsibility because of their ambiguity, but which nevertheless might be wrong under some other mode of responsibility?

5. Through the examples in this chapter an attempt is made to outline a consistent ethical position with regard to acts which threaten or destroy human life. Do you think the position is really consistent?

6. Some have argued that people necessarily intend all the aspects and results of their actions which they certainly foresee. Can you think of counterexamples to this contention?

7. At a number of points in the Bible, especially the Old Testament, God seems to be commanding someone to do something immoral. Assuming for the sake of argument that one takes these examples at their face value, is it possible to deal with the moral issue by using the theory of ambiguous action explained in this chapter?

8. Some argue that if war can ever be justified, the nuclear deterrent strategy intended to prevent war also can be justified. Do you agree?

9. If persons who do their best to do what they think is right avoid moral guilt anyway, why bother to make a close analysis of ambiguous actions? Why not instead simply tell people to follow their consciences when the time comes?

15: Our Development As Persons Depends on Us

Shifting responsibility is a game everyone feels tempted to play at times. People confronted with difficult jobs almost instinctively look about to see if they can find others to do the work for them. People confronting the disastrous results of jobs they have botched look instinctively for someone or something else to blame.

Built-in reluctance to accept responsibility is so much part of fallible human nature that it is not surprising to find it at work in regard to the fundamental task of every human being: determining what sort of persons we shall be. We are all responsible for our own development as persons, yet we are all tempted to shift the responsibility elsewhere and blame our failures on factors over which we have no control.

There are, as a matter of fact, good reasons for doing so—up to a point. In many respects our development as human beings does depend on factors beyond our control. These factors are of many different kinds, but basically they come down to only two: heredity and environment—the inbred characteristics transmitted to individuals by their parents and previous generations of forebears, and the circumstances of their lives and the world in which they live. Beyond doubt, influences from these sources do have a powerful impact in shaping and determining a human being. Beyond doubt, too, they are largely outside the control of the indi-

159

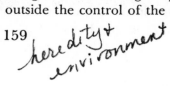

vidual, although in the case of environment not always totally so.

Having said this, however, one has only stated the obvious, without touching at all on the subject matter of ethics, the issue of freedom and its use. Granted, there are factors beyond our control which powerfully influence our development as human beings, but what of those factors which are *within* our power to control? There is the focal point of the challenge of freedom. And it is within this context that each one of us must work out his or her development, not merely as a human being but as a free, self-determining person.

Our development as persons depends strictly on the way in which we use our freedom. And the use of freedom is not determined by heredity and environment, the factors over which we have no control. On the contrary, precisely to the degree that our choices and actions are determined by these factors, freedom does not enter into the picture at all.

It is true that for many individuals the area within which they are able to exercise freedom is drastically reduced and in the case of some (those suffering from severe mental illness, for example) diminished almost to the vanishing point. But again, having said this, one has really said very little. Whatever degree of freedom an individual possesses, whether great or small, his or her development as a person depends on the use made of that freedom.

If John is "very free" (has many possibilities open to him), he has a corresponding opportunity to develop as a person on a wide front. If Jane is "hardly free at all," her opportunity to develop as a person is correspondingly limited. But to whatever extent John and Jane and the rest of us enjoy freedom, to precisely that extent each of us is responsible for our individual development according to the manner in which we use the freedom we have.

Ethics is not concerned with psychopathology or environmental limitations or with their consequences in human action. True, psychopathology and environmental limitations are facts of human life. But so is human freedom, and it is with freedom and its use that ethics is concerned.

People trying to live morally good lives may indeed find that factors over which they have no control interfere with their efforts. They may often find that they literally cannot do what they wish they could do. But their development as persons does not depend upon what they are truly unable to do (or, for that matter, unable to avoid doing) but rather upon that which they are able to do (or avoid doing). Their development as persons depends upon what they do with their freedom.

It should not be supposed that repeated failure in the attempt to do something indicates necessarily that the thing is impossible. Repeated failure may show that the thing is very difficult, but it may be that the experience of repeatedly trying—and failing—is precisely the process by which one eventually will achieve what one has in view. Even more to the point, it is precisely through this process of striving to achieve what is good (or, for that matter, what is bad) that self-determination comes into play and one shapes oneself as a person. Also, it is necessary to recognize the reality of conversion (not necessarily in a religious sense, although certainly that, too): a radical change in the orientation of one's life, quite possibly as the consequence of a long, although perhaps not fully conscious, process of striving for what is good, whereby the good which had previously seemed impossible of realization now becomes a realistic possibility. In short, it is important to distinguish what is truly impossible for one from what is only very difficult or is "impossible" at the moment but not necessarily for all time.

1. Moral Ideals

The most critical choice we make in life concerns the attitude we shall take toward moral ideals. It is critical because

on it depends our attitude toward and exercise of our freedom. On this choice, in other words, depends all of our moral
behavior, and thus our development as persons.

Moral standards are first presented to us in childhood—by
parents, teachers, peers, a host of other persons and influences. Typically, children accept moral standards on the basis
of authority. Their morality is a morality of obedience. To be
obedient is to be morally good. With time and maturity, however, individuals outgrow the simple equating of morality
with obedience. Then they must take the stance which will
govern their attitude toward moral ideals.

Two responses are possible. Aware perhaps that the moral
standards which they learned as children have imperfections
and limitations (may, in fact, be simply wrong), individuals
can nevertheless adopt an attitude of willingness to submit
themselves and their lives to more adequate moral
standards—standards which may have been refined and per-
fected by comparison with those of childhood but which are
real standards nevertheless.

Or, on the contrary, individuals can choose to regard
moral standards—any possible standards, not just those of
childhood—merely as facts with which they must contend as
they go about the business of getting what they want out of
life. People can, in other words, choose to approach moral
standards as the fundamental principles according to which
they will strive to shape their lives and themselves, or as external factors—no more important than many others—to be
manipulated according to their own preferences and inclinations.

Those who take the second attitude reject the task of developing as persons in favor of some more specific and
perhaps more immediately attractive goal or combination of
goals. They equivalently elect not to shape their lives by participating in fundamental goods constitutive of the human

person; instead they choose lives radically limited to the pursuit of specific objectives.

In doing so they also necessarily reject genuine community, in which mutual acceptance and respect are based on the embodiment of fundamental goods in other persons. They opt instead for what is at best a form of fragile coexistence with others, which threatens to break down whenever they find themselves thwarted in the pursuit of their objectives by the others' pursuit of *their* goals.

If, by contrast, people choose to submit themselves to moral ideals, they in fact commit themselves to accept the responsibility of freedom. They acknowledge that it is up to them to determine the persons they will be and that this will come about by the use they make of their freedom. In doing so, they do not automatically become complete persons. But they orient themselves in the direction—the only direction—which makes this possible.

Obviously the foregoing paragraphs suggest, as abstract presentations of living realities always do, that the process by which individuals arrive at their stance toward moral ideals is a mechanical, cut-and-dried business. In fact, it is quite otherwise. Growing children, for example, do not normally face the question of moral standards as such and abstractly. They encounter it in the concrete situations of daily life.

Faced with inner conflict—between the moral ideals with which they have been presented and the inclinations which tug at them to judge and act contrary to these standards—children gradually become aware that several quite different options are open to them. They may adhere to the standards they have received; they may seek standards which are, perhaps, similar but at the same time sounder; or else they may act simply on the basis of their own desires and inclinations, without deference to any principle standing over against them in judgment.

Similarly, adolescents (including persons who are morally adolescent but may, chronologically, be well beyond adolescence) frame the problem for themselves, not in terms of self-commitment and self-constitution, but in terms of authority, obedience, and a clash between the two. Typically, the tension in their lives is between doing as they please and doing as they have to do; and they think of what they "ought" to do as nothing more than one part—often a large and onerous part—of what they have to do.

→ Only gradually do people become able to remove the element of conflict and confrontation from their moral lives and achieve for themselves a stable reconciliation between those two poles: "what I want to do" and "what I have to do." Once an individual has reached this point, he or she has in effect reached moral maturity.

Even so, "moral maturity" does not necessarily mean the same thing as moral goodness. Morally mature people who are bad take account of what they have to do but live insofar as possible according to what they want to do. Morally mature persons who are good see that moral standards represent the possibilities of their own lives, the goods with which they can identify: they perceive that in acting for such goods they are in fact engaging in true self-determination or self-constitution.

Yet not even morally mature good persons have solved all their problems or reached a point at which the exercise of freedom of self-determination is easy and effortless. Human freedom always faces many obstacles—weakness, ignorance, the unsatisfactory character of the concrete circumstances in which we find ourselves—and we must contend with these if we wish to become morally better than we are.

There is no magic formula for dealing with the factors which obstruct the exercise of freedom. The best advice is common-sense advice. Ignorance can be reduced by reflection and study concerning the factors which bear upon one's life, by seeking and listening to the advice and counsel of others, and by periodic self-examination. Weakness can be lessened by learning to control one's emotions—not indeed by suppressing inclination but by using inclination to shape itself. If, for instance, fear of the consequences of doing something that should be done inclines one not to do it, one may find that attention to the good aspects of the matter—for example, the gratification to be expected from having done something which one considered right even though it was difficult—can stir up sufficient hope to overcome the fear.

The situations in which we find ourselves may often be beyond our power to control or alter significantly. At other times, however, at least some degree of control over situations may be within our power; and, still more often, we may be able to control the way in which we expose ourselves to situations. For example, a person struggling to cope with the fact of his or her alcoholism might at least be able to refrain from accompanying heavy-drinking friends on an evening of bar-hopping. In short, while the exercise of such qualities as honesty, objectivity, and prudence will not remove everything standing in the way of the exercise of freedom, it can do away with at least some obstacles and help to render others more or less manageable.

It is also important to bear in mind that in order to integrate one's commitments fully into the fabric of one's life, it is necessary to seek and perform a variety of actions which further and express the commitments in an expansive manner. Obviously, people who wish to further a commitment to the fundamental value of friendship will turn to the performance of kindly acts on behalf of those to whom they feel emotionally close—their "friends" in a narrow sense—but to achieve full self-integration, they must go further, expanding kindly acts beyond the circle of immediate friends so as to include persons who are not "friends" in the usual sense. Why does this foster self-integration? Because in dealing and seeking

ways to deal in a kindly fashion with such persons—casual
acquaintances, those with whom one is not on good terms,
and indeed everyone with whom one comes in contact—one
necessarily brings into play imagination, emotions, and other
faculties in support of the effort to find ways to express the
commitment and carry it out. And this is precisely the way in
which all of one's faculties come to be integrated around the
commitment.

Ultimately, our responsibility as free persons is very simple
and also very difficult. Simple to state and difficult, although
immensely rewarding, to carry out. It comes down to this: To
do the best we can to know what is right and the best we can to
do it, refusing to give up in the face of setbacks and failures,
however serious and frequent they may be.

Up to this point we have been concerned with laying out
the basic structure of an approach to ethics. Having sketched
its outlines in the preceding chapters, we have begun in this
chapter to suggest how it might be applied in concrete circumstances. The balance of this book will carry this effort further,
applying things already said to such matters as education,
social reform and revolution, theories of individual and social
progress, and the relationship of religion to morality.

Questions for Review and Discussion

1. This chapter begins a new section of the book. Can you sum-
marize what has been completed up to this point and indicate what is
now being undertaken?

2. We assume that heredity and environment can limit the possible exercise of freedom of self-determination. Identify some other
ways in which limitations on freedom are sometimes formulated and
expressed.

3. To what extent do you think you are free in comparison with
others of your own class and generation? in comparison with members of a primitive tribe? in comparison with the poorest classes of
our own society?

4. We describe in abstract language a fundamental option for or against moral ideals. Identify examples in fictional works in which such an option is being taken.

5. Is it in some sense a "reasonable" choice to choose against moral ideals? If so, is there any stronger reason for choosing in favor of them?

6. People who make a choice against moral ideals as the basis of their lives engage in a third-level act which puts them into the framework of second-level action. They remain there unless they alter their fundamental option. To what purpose are such persons committing themselves in their single, basic, third-level act?

7. It is frequently difficult for an adolescent to distinguish between the freedom of doing what one pleases and the freedom of self-determination. Why is this so?

8. We state that persons who make a basic option on the side of moral ideals must still contend with ignorance, weakness, and unsatisfactory situations if they are to become morally better. Illustrate concretely what these obstacles are in some actual cases and discuss ways in which they might be overcome.

9. To what extent and in what ways do you think ignorance, weakness, and unfavorable situations can limit or even eliminate moral guilt?

10. Discuss the logic of a person who argues as follows: "Nobody's perfect anyway, so it isn't so bad if now and then I do something I admit to be immoral."

11. Is it possible for someone to be a subjectivist in ethical theory and still make a consistent commitment on the side of moral ideals?

16: Shaping the Future

Social reformers, bent on changing the world for the sake of a cause, almost always turn their sights eventually on children. The young are the hope of the future. Not yet corrupted, not yet morally evil, they represent the opportunity to make a fresh start.

The very receptiveness of children to external influences supports this view of them. Unlike adults, who seem relatively set in their ways, children can be shaped and changed, both intellectually and morally. Seemingly discernible in them is the chance to create a world from which the failings and blemishes of the present have been eradicated. Thus the education of children is seen as the key to the future.

This view of education or formation is plausible and by no means entirely wrong. Education, broadly considered, can indeed play a powerful role in the formation of the young, including their moral development. But we must be realistic and not overstate the case. The potential—of the child on the one hand and any educational system on the other—is limited. With particular reference to our subject, it is not possible for any system of formation or education to *make* children morally good, since moral goodness or badness is a matter of *self*-determination.

An educational system can make it easier or more difficult for children to be morally good. It can create conditions under which children, now and in the future, are somewhat more likely to choose rightly. But that is all it can do. There is no failure-proof formula for raising children in a way which will guarantee that they will be morally good adults. Given the reality of what it means to be morally good, there can be none.

Not every theory of education acknowledges that this is so. In fact, some ideas about education are based on the contrary assumption: that it is possible to make children morally good. In general, such educational theories have mistaken notions about morality itself. It is worth examining some of these theories briefly, both in order to see where they go wrong and also as a prelude to considering what can be accomplished through the education of children.

Commonplace at present, as it has also been at times in the past, is the idea that children are naturally good and therefore need only to be allowed to do as they please in order to grow up as morally good persons. Immorality is seen as something which comes to them from outside. But if they are permitted simply to follow their own instincts, they will spontaneously do what is morally right.

This view would be correct if human beings were simply animals, since an animal which does what its instincts dictate is doing what is right for it as an animal. But human beings are not simply animals, and human morality is a good deal more complex. Permissiveness in itself does nothing to prepare a child for self-determination, which lies at the heart of adult morality. On the contrary, its likely result is to leave the child singularly ill-equipped to function in an authentically self-determining manner in later life.

Another approach holds that moral evil is at bottom a matter of ignorance. If therefore children are well informed, if they know the facts, they will act intelligently and thus morally. One can agree that there is no value in having people misinformed and that it is desirable for them to be well informed. But being well informed is just not the same thing as being morally good. While ignorance is not a virtue, neither is knowledge.

People who are well informed can put their knowledge to morally good uses or to morally bad ones. A master criminal is not a morally good person simply because of high intelligence and the command of a wide range of information. The Faust legend dramatizes the obvious fact that knowledge is one thing and moral goodness something else again.

Another theory holds that evil arises from society—from other people—and that children can therefore be protected from evil by being isolated from its carriers. There is certainly more than a grain of truth in this: no sensible person wishes gratuitously to expose children to evil people.

At the same time, however, this view goes wrong when, as often happens, evil is identified obsessively and almost exclusively with one group (the "Communists" or the "capitalists," the "blacks" or the "whites," etc.) and it is assumed that segregating the child from the group thus identified as evil is a guarantee that the child will be morally good. Also, while it is reasonable to keep children from people who are really evil, this does not offer any ironclad assurance that they will exercise their own power of self-determination in a morally good way.

A fourth theory suggests that if people are compelled to act in morally good ways when they are young, they will continue to do what is good when they are adults. Simply put, this is a theory of good habits. But everything we have seen about moral maturity up to now underlines the fact that the moral goodness of an adult is a matter not of habit and routine but of correct, free, self-determining choice.

Good habits are unquestionably desirable, for both children and adults, and we may be morally responsible for our bad habits. But good habits are not identical with good morality; indeed, an action performed simply out of habit, if there ever is such a thing, has of itself no particular moral quality—good or bad—at all. The moral quality resides in our efforts to keep or alter our habits.

Each of these educational/formational theories goes wrong in overlooking the fact that moral goodness and moral evil result from self-determination. Moral goodness cannot be guaranteed or moral evil eradicated by education. Human beings retain the power to dispose of their own lives, for good or ill, regardless of the educational system to which they have been exposed. And to the extent that education might deprive an individual of the capacity for self-determination, it would also drain his or her life of moral quality.

Even if the science-fiction dream of some determinists were realized—a system of education which would condition individuals always to do what is right—the result would be far removed from a situation in which everyone was, in the full sense of the words, "morally good." In such circumstances people's actions would have no more moral quality, good or bad, than the behavior of obedient animals or well-programmed machines. The recalcitrant persistence of human freedom suggests, however, that no such system is likely soon to become reality.

1. What Education Can Do

Having seen what education cannot accomplish as far as morality is concerned, it is time now to turn to the more important question of what it can do—but with a constant awareness, assumed in all that follows, of its limits, which are essentially two: heredity and environment. About heredity it can do nothing. About environment it can do something—perhaps a good deal; yet no practically conceivable system of education can hope to control the vast multitude of factors which go to make up a child's environment, and most systems are practically capable of touching only a highly restricted segment of the child's total environment.

Nevertheless, although education cannot guarantee morally good behavior in either the child or the adult, it can at least do some things which will tend to make it easier for the child and the adult to choose and do what is morally right.

First, education must recognize in confronting children that, in regard to morality as well as other matters, they *are* children and not miniature adults. It is a mistake to suppose that a young child is capable of self-determination in the same way as a morally mature adult.

Although children do make choices in a sense, they are not aware of themselves as self-determining and are therefore incapable of full self-determination. Morally speaking, they are at a stage where obedience or its contrary is the dominant factor, and necessarily so. Thus it is essential that sound rules be formulated and enforced to govern their behavior. No one responsible for their education should have to apologize for doing so.

At the same time rules for children must meet various criteria. They should be consistent, since otherwise they embody some irrationality and cannot really be followed. Like any good system of law, the rules should also be clear, since otherwise children cannot tell what is expected of them (and cannot in fairness be punished for failing to do it). The rules should be oriented to purposes and goals which make sense—and whose sense is pointed out and explained to the children in terms they are able to understand. And the rules should be nonexploitative.

Too many rule-systems for children are, in fact, designed for the benefit of adults—parents or teachers—and are not really in the best interests of the children at all. Ideally, a set of nonexploitative moral rules for children will be made up of

rules which they would set for themselves if they were able—
if, that is, they were fully self-determining and bent on doing
what is morally right.

If the rule-system is developed in this way, it will be possible for individuals, as they mature, to incorporate essentially
the same rules—albeit, in many cases more sophisticated
versions—into their lives. Thus, instead of having to make a
sharp transition from childhood morality to adult morality,
individuals experience their moral lives as a continuum in
which they achieve deeper insight into moral principles
rather than abandoning old principles in favor of new ones.

At the same time, while providing moral rules for children,
an educational system must take care not to overorganize
their lives. It is extremely important that there be free areas
dispersed throughout the day in which, acting within the general framework of the rules, the child is nevertheless free to
investigate and experiment in making choices among various
goods.

It is a mistake for parents and teachers rigidly to plan and
organize all of children's time for them, even though they
may be tempted to do this "for their own good." Children
need the opportunity for free and spontaneous activity,
within a system of rules, and this is extremely important to
their moral development.

During free areas which they share with adults children are
introduced noncoercively to goods to which it is worthwhile to
commit themselves. They are given the opportunity of sharing in the committed activity of adults engaged in doing
something which is valuable for its own sake.

This is not simply a matter of togetherness or even of
adults giving good example to children. The point, rather, is
that children learn what commitment to human goods means
by seeing adults performing actions which express their
commitment and by having an opportunity to share in such

activity—without, however, being pressured to do so. In this way a simple family outing, during which the parents genuinely relax and enjoy themselves and the children are invited to share in the enjoyment, can teach children much more than any number of words what "participation in the good of play" is all about.

Equally important are the free areas which the child shares with other children, which in our society are generally grouped under the label of "playing." To an adult a child's play may seem more or less meaningless activity, but it has a crucial role in the child's moral development. In play situations with other children the child develops a sense of fairness and justice and comes to appreciate the need for authority within relationships which are nonexploitative and nonpaternalistic.

Finally, children need free areas by themselves: periods in which they have opportunity to reflect, dream, and seek themselves in forms of activity in which they engage for no other reason except that they enjoy and value them. Such periods are, in effect, occasions to prepare for and rehearse the acts of self-determination by which they will constitute themselves as persons.

One of the much-debated questions about the raising of children is whether and when to use force. Force must sometimes be employed to prevent the child from doing what is wrong. Force intended to compel a child to do what is right is, at best, meaningless as far as making any contribution to moral maturity is concerned. For in terms of moral maturity it is only the good which one elects to do—not the good which one is compelled to do—which has value.

Forcing a child to do good things can actually have negative results in the long run. The child who is coerced to spend half an hour a day practicing the piano may very well grow up with an aversion to music; it is much more likely that a child who has been encouraged but not compelled to take pleasure in music will grow up as an adult capable of freely appreciating the good of which music is an expression.

In short, moral rules and the enforcement of those rules for children should be mainly negative: directed at preventing children from doing what is wrong rather than compelling them to do what is right. Good which is done as a result of compulsion provides at best a shaky foundation for later virtue.

The moral education of children also requires that their emotions be educated. It is extremely important that they be helped to develop hope: an attitude based on the belief that things which are hard but worthwhile can be accomplished. This can be done by encouraging them to undertake tasks which are difficult but possible.

If things are always too easy for children, they have no need to hope, and they will be unprepared for later challenges which are not easy at all. If, on the other hand, things are too difficult—if they are consistently frustrated by failing at the tasks which are set for them—they are likely to conclude that no amount of effort is ever likely to produce good results and to adopt an attitude of despair.

Furthermore, it is wise to encourage children to strive for goals in areas in which they are interested (sports, hobbies, etc.) even if these may seem frivolous and trivial to some adults. So far as moral development is concerned, what is at stake is the maturing of a particular attitude rather than the acquisition of useful skills or social graces.

The child should also be helped to develop self-control. This is not done by threats and punishment but by proposing a self-ideal: "Isn't this what you really want to do and to be? Then in order to accomplish it, this is what you must do." Success in living up to the self-ideal proposed is praised and rewarded. Thus the child is given support and encouragement in overcoming emotional barriers and fitting actions to the self-ideal.

As children's ability to understand grows, they must be given reasons for the moral rules which have been set for them. The reasons given should be the real ones—framed, of course, in concepts and language they are able to grasp. Children should also be included in the process by which important family decisions are reached. The making of the decisions should not be turned over to them, but they should be exposed to the deliberative activity by which adults arrive maturely at important decisions and should be allowed, to the extent of their growing competence, to contribute to it.

It is also important that children have companions who share the same moral framework and outlook on life. This does not imply some sort of invidious segregation—racial, religious, economic, or whatever—which would in fact be highly undesirable even if it were hypothetically possible in a particular case. The point, rather, is that children should have the opportunity to be part of a community of children whose value-system is the same and who, within the framework of that value system, can proceed autonomously to develop their own rules and structures.

Providing such a setting is, generally, not too difficult in large families, where brothers and sisters tend spontaneously to create a community whose members share the same values and moral framework. Today, however, this can be a much more difficult thing: families are smaller and schools and neighborhoods are usually quite heterogeneous. Thus special effort and ingenuity on the part of parents may be required to see to it that children do in fact have the opportunity of associating with other children who share the same moral standards. The effort is, however, well worth making because of the importance of this factor in moral development.

Finally, a word about religious training. It is a mistake to suppose that one can make children good by making them religious, and the mistake lies basically in the fact that this degrades religion by making it an instrument of morality. This is reflected in the attitude of parents who say, "We send

Johnny to Sunday school to be sure he gets some moral training." Religion should be presented to children as something
which is valuable and important in itself, not as an adjunct of
good moral behavior.

True, most religious systems do demand a moral commitment on the part of the individual adherent. But in this case
the adherents want, presumably, to behave in a morally correct manner because of their religious beliefs: they seek to be
moral because they want to be holy rather than the other way
around.

The ideal of sanctity, as a function of religion, can indeed
be a powerful inducement to moral behavior on the part of
one who accepts the ideal. But neither holiness nor ethical
goodness is likely to be served by confusing the two things and
attempting to use religion or religious training as a means to
induce good behavior on the part of the child.

Nor can religious training be merely a matter of brainwashing and indoctrination. Religion, grounded ultimately on
convictions about the reality of a transcendent Other with
whom or which it is important to be in a proper relationship,
should be presented to the child as an alternative to the world
view of egoism, in which the rest of the world is seen as revolv-
ing around oneself. Religious transcendence does have powerful ethical implications, reinforcing and validating as it does
the willingness of individuals to submit themselves to values
and standards beyond themselves. This view of religion, however, is hardly likely to come across to the child in a setting in
which religion itself is reduced to the role of a handmaid of
good moral behavior.

We cannot end this part of our exposition without pointing
out again that the suggestions we have advanced, like the
suggestions of others, do not guarantee the moral progress of
individuals and society as a whole. There can be no such
guarantees as long as human freedom remains a reality. In
the chapter which follows we shall examine in greater detail
what this means.

Questions for Review and Discussion

1. Think of examples from your experience of educational practices which seemed to be based on the various theories of education mentioned near the beginning of this chapter. In your opinion how did these practices work out?

2. Can you think of reasons why so many approaches to education seem to be based on a denial—at least in practice—of freedom of self-determination?

3. The theories of education which we reject are not normally presented as alternatives to a philosophy of education based on freedom of self-determination. Research educational theory a bit and see how such theories are presented.

4. As long as substantive human goods are actually realized, does it really make any difference whether or not action is done by freedom of self-determination? If so, what difference?

5. Think of examples of rules made by adults to govern the behavior of children. Criticize these examples according to the criteria suggested.

6. In what sense of "freedom" are the free areas of a child's life free?

7. Do you think the lives of most children today are overorganized? What do you think of the fact that many children spend a great part of their free time watching television?

8. In relationships of adults with children what subtle forms of force are often employed to try to compel them to do what is good?

9. Gather information about institutions for delinquent children. To what extent are such institutions likely to cultivate an attitude of hope? How could they do so?

10. How does the proposal that children be assured companions who share the same value framework differ from a proposal to practice segregation?

11. If you have experienced religious education, discuss the extent to which it may have confused the religious with the ethical.

12. Show how the theory of education proposed in the present chapter is based on considerations in chapter fifteen.

17: Progress in Perspective

Back in the 1920s a popular charlatan encouraged people to psych themselves by repeating regularly "Every day in every way I'm getting better and better." Foolish as the phrase sounds now, it epitomizes an enduring phenomenon: the notion that human progress is continuous and inevitable.

This belief in the inevitability of progress has been expressed in many different ways throughout history. Two of these are important in the contemporary world: Marxism and a vulgarized version of evolutionary theory.

Adopting a pseudoscientific approach, the dialectical view of history espoused by orthodox Marxists attempts to lay down firm predictions regarding the historical process. The difficulty is that its predictions concerning the inevitable march of events have not been borne out by the facts. This point has been discussed at length by critics of Marxism, and there is no need to repeat at length here what has been said elsewhere. It is simply a fact that history has not turned out the way it should according to the dialectic of Marx and Engels.

As far as evolutionary theory is concerned, it is necessary to distinguish between biological evolutionism and evolution loosely conceived as an optimistic philosophy of progress. As a biological hypothesis accounting for the variety of types of organic life, evolutionary theory makes no pretense of

179

guaranteeing inevitable progress. The process of selection merely determines that some kinds of life will survive and others will die off, not that this will necessarily represent qualitative advancement. One can easily imagine a state of affairs in which human beings could no longer survive on the earth but in which insects continued to survive and flourish. The cockroach, in that case, could be the "highest" form of life.

Nevertheless, some philosophers, notably Herbert Spencer in the nineteenth century, attempted to translate evolutionism into a comprehensive theory of progress. Spencer was hailed in his day as a great thinker, but little is heard of him now. The reason is obvious. The First and Second World Wars, the Great Depression, Auschwitz, the Stalinist terror, Hiroshima and Nagasaki, Vietnam—these and many other vast calamities of the twentieth century have made it all but impossible for intelligent people to swallow the idea that the progress of the human race in history is in any way guaranteed.

Indeed, the overriding fact of contemporary history is that the human race, far from having moved steadily forward, now confronts the appalling possibility of wiping itself off the face of the earth. This is not what most people mean by progress.

1. Is Progress Possible?

On the other hand, it is clear enough that humanity has indeed made real progress in many fields over the centuries. Progress is apparent in such areas as theoretical knowledge and technology. Indeed, it is only in virtue of progress in these areas that the human race now has the capability of destroying itself. But the progress involved here might more correctly be described as accumulation. In mathematics, for example, a reasonably apt student can now accomplish things far beyond what Euclid was capable of. Mathematicians now know more than Euclid did and are therefore able to do more than he could do. This truly is progress of a sort.

Progress exists in philosophy, too. Not that the basic philosophical problems have been finally resolved or are likely to be. Rather, over the course of centuries certain solutions have come to be seen as unacceptable. At least the philosopher now knows that some answers to some questions, which at one time seemed plausible to reasonable people, are simply invalid and untenable. This also represents progress.

Technological progress is an overwhelming fact of life today. There was, after all, a time in the history of the human race when people did not know the use of the wheel and of fire. Now people travel to the moon and split the atom as a source of energy.

Similarly, there is a kind of progress in the fine arts. This is not to say that Picasso is a greater painter than Botticelli, or Stravinsky a finer composer than Bach. But the painter today commands certain techniques—methods of pigmentation and perspective, for instance—which were unknown to painters a thousand years ago; today's musicians have a far wider range of sounds at their disposal, thanks to the development of modern instruments and electronic devices, than Renaissance composers did. As a result of improved technique, today's painter and composer can *do* things which painters and composers of earlier centuries could not do. Moreover, apart from accidental losses, the creative accomplishments of previous ages remain available for us to admire and, if we wish, to imitate, while our artists go on in the attempt to set new standards of creativity. While much of what they do will fall away, some of it will become part of the cultural heritage of later generations.

This list can be extended. Men and women today—at least in many parts of the world—are physically larger and stronger than their ancestors, enjoy better health, and live longer. They have more leisure and also have greater access to resources for play, aesthetic experience, and intellectual pursuits. All this, too, represents progress.

But the progress involved is essentially one of accumulation. People are able to do more—to realize certain goods more fully. This, however, does not imply that they live morally better lives. The accumulation of skills and techniques, of tools and technologies, makes it theoretically possible for people to do more moral good; it also makes it just as possible for them to do more moral evil.

In short, the kind of progress achieved by the human race up to now offers no grounds for assuming the inevitability of moral progress. It only means that over the centuries there has been an expansion of human ability to do both good and evil.

This has not always been clear to modern thinkers and is not clear to all of them today. More than fifty years ago John Dewey, noting the fact of technological progress, complained that the social sciences had lagged behind the natural sciences and suggested that something could and should be done about this. Dewey believed that the moral dimension of human life should be susceptible to external control, more or less as technology had been brought to bear in the solution of physical problems. For example, supposing we fully understood the causes of crime, it ought to be possible to devise and apply techniques which would eradicate or at least effectively control the criminal propensities in people.

The difficulty with this view, however, is that it fails to recognize the radical difference between human action and technique. Techniques aim to achieve specific, concrete objectives; they fail only by error or accident. But human action as such—that is, action which is free—aims at open-ended ideals and fails precisely because of a failure of choice: because, that is, people choose to settle for limited goals and, in doing so, close themselves off from other possibilities whose realization would make them more fully human.

Suppose for a moment the hypothetical possibility of devising a human technology which would indeed somehow make it impossible to make morally evil choices. Denied the opportunity of choosing wrongly, we would in fact be denied the opportunity of choosing freely. And in the absence of freedom human life would no longer have any moral quality. Because action was no longer free, it would be neither morally good nor morally bad.

A human technology (some kind of super psychic conditioning or brainwashing, for instance) might—again hypothetically—eliminate moral evil from human life, but it would do so at the cost of simultaneously eliminating moral goodness. It would achieve its end by reducing the person to the status of an object, to be manipulated by "experts," persons of presumably superior and virtually superhuman wisdom and moral rectitude.

The only conclusion from all this is that as far as morality is concerned, there is no such thing as necessary and inevitable progress. As long as human beings are free, and to the extent that they are free, they retain a dual capacity for moral good and moral evil. They are able to choose well or badly. Only by eliminating freedom could one eliminate the possibility of people choosing evil; in the process one would also eliminate the possibility of their freely choosing good.

This is not a pessimistic view of human beings. It does not say that life goes around in circles or that each generation is condemned to repeat the mistakes of previous generations. But neither does it say that the course of history is necessarily forward and upward. Rather, the pattern of history presents a broken front: some progress in some areas at some times, together with regression in other areas at the same time. Such a view is neither pessimistic nor optimistic; it is simply realistic.

It may be objected that in our times there are signs that the human race is indeed capable not simply of spotty and uncertain moral progress but of genuine moral breakthroughs. The weakening of nationalism—which has been the cause of so much conflict and suffering in history—is cited as one example. So is the disappearance in most places of slavery.

Yet the decline of nationalism (to the extent that it really has declined) can be seen as a mere by-product of improvements in communications techniques and the development of new technology drawing people more closely together. The virtual disappearance of slavery can be attributed to the fact that it is only economically practical in agricultural societies, whereas modern societies are increasingly industrialized.

In short, these and other developments in our times do not reflect steadily evolving moral progress but point only to the fact that archaic practices and abuses are generally discontinued as they become less useful. Furthermore, without belaboring the point, it is difficult to make a compelling argument for steady and inevitable moral progress in the age of Auschwitz, the nuclear deterrent, and widespread abortion-on-request.

2. The Search for Panaceas

Confronting the fact that a realistic view of history and the human condition gives no ground for optimism about the inevitability of moral progress, people at various times have come up with panaceas intended to remove the obstacles to such progress and insure it in the future. We shall take note of four here: the psychoanalytic panacea, the new morality panacea, the panacea of new institutions and new communities, and the religious panacea.

The psychoanalytic panacea, a complex of psychological and sociological notions based loosely on the theories of Freud and others, reduces evil to illness. People have hang-ups—mental and emotional quirks—which cause them to act badly. If they can be cured of these, and if techniques of child-raising and education can be devised which prevent their recurrence in future generations, the cause of evil will be eliminated and human beings will be good.

It is true that emotional illness is a reality, and it is also true that some emotional illnesses can be cured or at least alleviated by psychoanalysis or other forms of therapy. But it is not true that if people are released from their psychic hang-ups, they will then necessarily do what is right. On the contrary, if a person is really made more free by therapy, his or her capacity for free choice—of evil as well as good—is thereby increased. Curing people of neuroses may make them healthy, but it does not guarantee that they will be morally good.

The new-morality approach argues that the old morality kept people in bondage and made them hypocrites. Now, however, we are to enjoy a morality of freedom. Human beings have come of age, and they will henceforth act maturely and responsibly. The treatment in the preceding chapters of the responsibilities of freedom indicates the extent to which there is something valid in the claims of the new morality but also underlines the fact that freedom to do as one pleases is not the same as freedom of self-determination.

Unfortunately for the high hopes placed by some in the new morality, new moralities have come along with depressing regularity over the centuries, always making the same claims to liberate humanity and usher in a new age. It has not happened yet, and, on the evidence, there is no reason to suppose it will happen in the future.

The panacea of institutional reform attributes evil to institutions, which are said to distort and corrupt human relationships. Change—or perhaps do away with—institutions, create new communities, adopt new patterns of human relationships, and people will cease to do evil and become universally good and loving and generous. As we have seen, large societies always are a mixture of community and exploitation; perhaps small communes based on immediate interpersonal relationship—and excluding anyone over thirty—will do better.

While it is true that many institutions are corrupt and all are imperfect, the evidence of history shows, once again, that it is naive to expect much in this direction. Movements of institutional reform (or revolution) have recurred repeatedly and, just as repeatedly, have failed to bring about the promised golden age. Indeed, the evidence suggests that it is generally wiser to attempt to build on the basis of whatever community exists within present institutions rather than tear down existing institutions and communities in the hope that what comes after will be better than what went before. The average life expectancy of a commune, we are told, is a couple of months.

The religious panacea, finally, comes in two forms: on the one hand, the religion or religions we have had until now have failed us, and we must therefore have a new religion; on the other, all religion is a snare and a delusion, distracting people from their proper area of concern in this world and placing them in thrall to myths and to a priestly caste bent on perpetuating those myths—and so, for human beings to be freed from superstition in order to pursue their proper destiny, religion itself must be done away with.

Each of these pseudosolutions to the problem of human happiness and goodness has enjoyed popularity at various times in history, and both have a certain vogue at the present moment. Yet neither solution has contributed anything very tangible to the improvement of human life, and taken together, they simply cancel eath other out. Partisans of religion may look back to the "age of faith" as a high-point in human history, conveniently forgetting the Inquisition and the wars of religion; partisans of modern secularism may bask in the glow of the "enlightenment," conveniently forgetting that totalitarian ideologies have replaced ancient theologies and that the earthly paradise of unlimited consumption has brought the world's wealthiest nation to the point where it is smothering under its own nuclear, chemical, and organic wastes.

At bottom, all of these panaceas are based on the conviction that human beings are not really free and that, therefore, the source of moral goodness and moral evil lies outside their self-determination. Yet the thrust of everything we have said comes down to this: human beings are free, human beings are self-determining, and human beings make themselves good or evil according to their own free choice. If that is so, there is and can be no such thing as inevitable moral progress on the part of the human race.

Progress is possible for us individually and together if we choose it. But to say it is possible for us to make moral progress is not at all the same as saying it is inevitable that we will do so. We are free to choose well, to make choices by which we realize more fully what it means to be human. But because we are free, we can also choose badly, opting if we wish for growing depersonalization and inhumanity. There is no inevitability here; in a true and profound sense it is up to us to make of ourselves, individually and together, what we choose to be.

Questions for Review and Discussion

1. We deal here only in passing with Marxism. Investigate other aspects of this philosophy as a theory of progress. Consider other criticisms proposed against the philosophy and also other aspects of Marxism which make it as attractive as it obviously is to many people.

2. In what sense does biological evolution guarantee the "survival of the fittest"? To what extent does the concept of evolution change as it is applied in other areas of the natural sciences, e.g., the evolution of the physical universe? To the social sciences, e.g., cultural evolution?

3. Has progress in science and technology been constant throughout history? How can it be accounted for?

4. To what extent would a morally good person be intent upon furthering progress in the areas in which progress is possible?

5. Explain the relationship between Dewey's attitude toward progress and his theory of situationism, discussed in chapter ten.

6. Do you know of any theories in psychology that propose to produce good people by a process of human engineering?

7. List present-day phenomena that might be used to argue either for or against the occurrence of moral progress. Apart from the theoretical consideration that human beings have freedom of self-determination, do you see any strong reasons for arguing either for or against the proposition that moral progress occurs?

8. Do you know of—or can you find examples of—the positions on progress we regard here as panaceas? What is there about each of these positions that makes it plausible to intelligent people?

9. Any theory which holds moral progress to be inevitable excludes freedom of self-determination. But proponents of such theories often argue that the end of progress will be precisely freedom, or increasing freedom. "Freedom" in what sense or senses?

18: Revolution and Reform

(handwritten margin note:) ① Exploitive ✓ ② Contractual ✓ ③ Communitarian ✓

What role ought revolution and reform to play in making human society more just and more virtuous? The issue is particularly pressing today, when revolution is frequently invoked as not only a solution but the sole solution to evil and injustice in society. And it is closely linked to the whole question of whether and how moral progress is possible.

The problem is a complicated one. There are three quite different kinds of relationships among people—exploitative, contractual, and communitarian—and all three are generally found not merely side by side but intertwined in any large and complex society. Since the relationships are different, the remedies to abuses will also be different; yet because the relationships coexist in the same society, a solution which from one perspective might be appropriate to correct an abuse may, considered in the light of a different form of relationship, be inappropriate and even harmful.

Thus, while violent revolution may be urged as the proper solution to abuses of an exploitative nature, we must also recognize that revolution is likely to destroy such elements of community as do exist within a society. In such circumstances it is not easy to know how to proceed in order to remedy the situation.

As in the case of individual evil, so also in the case of evil in

189

society a number of false or at best partial solutions are proposed. On the analogy that society is an organism, social evil is explained as a sort of disease, a form of social pathology. Or evil is ascribed to a lack of communication; presumably, if people and groups communicate more freely and fully with one another, social evils will disappear. Another theory attributes the evil in society to a particular class or group: the capitalists or the Communists, the blacks or the whites, the rebellious young or the hypocritical middle-aged, and so forth. In still another view, social evil is the fruit of bad institutions—institutions which are too large and impersonal; salvation is seen to lie in small groups, various types of minisociety regarded as more conducive to community.

Each of these explanations locates the cause of evil in society elsewhere than in self-determination. But as we have stressed repeatedly, *moral* evil is precisely the result of self-determination. Unquestionably, societies do suffer from other ills than those which can be described as moral ones, and to the extent that this may be true in a given society, each of the explanations noted above may have validity. But to the extent that the evil in society is really moral evil, no explanation or solution which fails to see that moral evil is rooted in self-determination can be considered realistic. And explanations which are unrealistic in this matter will be unlikely to contribute to the eradication of social evil even to the extent that such evil may be due to factors other than the moral one.

The only remedy for the abuse of human freedom is the proper use of freedom. This immediately suggests that there are social evils to which there is no social solution: objectively bad situations which there is, realistically speaking, no way of rectifying by any means—or at least any legitimate means—accessible to society as such. Failure to acknowledge that freedom exists or that it is sometimes abused leads either to a dead-end street or to the adoption of coercive and very likely unfruitful measures for correcting moral evil—in society as well as in the individual. In saying this, we are not writing off the possibility of individual and social reform; we are only stating a necessary and important caution with regard to means and expectations.

1. Social Relationships

The problems which arise in each of the three kinds of social relationship are different, as also are their remedies. We shall look briefly at each in order to see what avenues of redress are open to those who suffer injury as a result of someone else's misuse of freedom.

If the relationship is exploitative, the obvious solution for those who are exploited is to gain enough power to change the relationship to a contractual one, in which both sides (or all sides) derive roughly equal benefits. If the exploitation exists within a larger society where there is a common authority, the exploited can appeal to that authority to correct the abuse and right the balance. (In the United States, for instance, this presumably is one of the crucial functions of a body such as the Supreme Court.) Finally, as a last resort, the exploited individual or group can employ physical force in an effort to halt the exploitation. Realistically, however, there is a good chance that a resort to force will not succeed if the exploiters have made an accurate calculation of the relative power available to themselves on the one hand and the exploited on the other.

If physical violence is used, it is equivalently warfare, and the same stringent limitations on the use of force in war which were noted earlier must be observed. Rebellion can only be justified as warfare is; one is not permitted to do something immoral to rectify injustice. Furthermore, it should be clear that revolution in this case is not "revolution" in the same sense in which that word is often used at the present time. Contemporary prophets of revolution give the term an almost mystical meaning, using it to describe some sort of fundamental transformation in human beings and human relationships. But revolution—the use of physical force—intended simply to end an exploitative relationship does not involve any such fundamental transformation; it is merely the direct use of force to counter unjust force being used for exploitation.

A contractual relationship stands midway between exploitation and community. It can be described as a kind of benign, mutual exploitation: each party gives up something to the other or others in order to get something in return. In a fair contractual relationship that which each surrenders is roughly comparable in value to that which each receives. However, an initially just contractual relationship can degenerate into a sort of sanctioned exploitation when one of the parties begins to give less and get more.

This can come about in either of two ways: either one of the parties more or less deliberately violates the terms of the contract or else the conditions to which the contract applies change significantly, so that the balance shifts and one party finds himself or herself having to give a great deal and receiving very little, while the other gives very little and receives a great deal. When a contractual relationship changes in this way, it ceases in fact to be a contract and becomes ordinary exploitation.

That being so, the means of redress are those outlined above when exploitation occurs: appeal by the injured party to the sense of justice of the exploiter, appeal to an authority which has power to enforce contracts, and in extreme cases recourse to violence in order to counter the violence of the exploiter. The moral problem as far as resort to violence is concerned is that often there is no act which the exploited can do that will in and of itself lessen the violence being done to them; violence, therefore, is likely to be a means to an ulterior end and is morally excluded for that reason.

When a contract is violated by one party, the injured party is of course no longer morally obliged to observe its terms— but this is often of little help. For injured parties in such cases either frequently have already carried out their part of the contractual arrangement or in many cases can be made to suffer more loss than gain if they fail to do so, even though it is not just that they should *have* to do so.

Still, there is reason to think that it is generally less difficult to correct exploitation resulting from a contractual relationship which has gone sour than it is to rectify an exploitative situation in which nothing but exploitation was ever involved. For in the case of what started out as a contract there was at least an initial commitment on both sides to a rough kind of equity, and if this commitment has not entirely vanished, it may be possible to reconstruct the relationship on its basis.

At the same time, however, contract is a more impersonal kind of relationship than either direct exploitation or community. It is arguable, for instance, that some nineteenth-century plantation slaves enjoyed a more "human" relationship with their owners than did some nineteenth-century factory workers with the owners of their factories. One consequence of this is that a contractual relationship can become and remain exploitative without direct ill will on anyone's part but simply as a result of changed circumstances which no one anticipated or particularly intended.

This suggests that in a concrete situation of mixed exploitation and community—a real-life situation which one encounters with some frequency—it may not be advisable to attempt to change the relationship to a purely contractual one. Instead, it may be better in particular cases to seek to correct the situation by building upon such elements of community as

already exist rather than eliminating community along with
exploitation by making the relationship exclusively contractual.

For example, the solution to the problems of a family in
which the parents, although basically loving, are habitually
exploitative of their children might better be sought in counseling, encouragement, and mutual efforts at understanding
and charity than in legal action, which can end by separating
the children from their parents and making them wards of
the state.

As we have seen, communities are based on a shared commitment by their members to the mutual realization of some
fundamental good or goods. Communities can go wrong in
their constituting act (the original Constitution of the United
States, for example, made provision for slavery), in the institutions which express constitutional purposes, or in particular actions. The institutions of a community are corrupt
when, as a result either of design or accident, they embody
exploitation.

Tax loopholes which unjustly favor some individuals or
groups at the expense of others are a good example of this. In
some cases tax breaks may originally have had a justification,
but over a period of time many such arrangements have become
simply means by which some members of the community are required to pay for the special privileges which others enjoy; in
other cases the loopholes may have been unjust from the
start: they were never anything but a kind of institutionalized
exploitation hiding behind the facade of law.

Finally, the injustice which exists in communities as a result
of particular actions comes about when individuals fail to
carry out the duties which are properly theirs by reason of
their roles in society. As we have seen, an individual faced
with a genuine conflict of duties may morally be excused from
performing some of them. But an individual cannot consistently claim the benefits of membership in particular societies

and neglect the duties which arise from such membership without being guilty of injustice and irresponsibility.

2. Reform of Community

Given the nature of a community, the only way to correct evil compatible with the principle of community itself is through communication, persuasion, an appeal to reason and good will (not excluding an appeal to emotion). Community can never be maintained by force, because the use of force by some members of the community against others is inherently destructive of community.

If, then, individuals in a community are guilty of evil actions contrary to the commitments which bind the community together, one must appeal to the institutions which embody the community's purposes in an effort to persuade such persons to live up to the duties which those institutions impose. And if the institutions themselves embody evil and injustice, one must appeal to the constitutional principles of the community in order to have the institutions brought into conformity with those purposes.

It is of course possible to use force at the operational level, and it may even be necessary at times to do so: for instance, people who break the law must sometimes be arrested and imprisoned. At the institutional level it is also possible to play politics (operate within the framework of the institutions as they are) in an effort to achieve an advantageous result without correcting what is wrong with the institutions. But to the extent that either of these things—using force, playing politics—is done, the principle of community has been abandoned, and the relationship has been forced into the pattern of either exploitation or contract.

Where problems within a community concern fundamental constitutional principles, the methods for tackling the difficulty must be essentially philosophic. One may, for example, attempt to demonstrate to other members of the community that a particular part of the constitution is inconsistent with other principles embodied there: for instance, toleration of slavery cannot very well coexist with commitment to the principle that human beings are fundamentally equal and possess equal rights.

If, however, there is no demonstrable urgency and the constituting principles are in fact mutually consistent, the only recourse is an appeal to basic principles of right and wrong which should govern action independently of any other commitments. Admittedly, the chances of success in such circumstances are not great. When the members of a community are bent on doing what is wrong, arguments intended to point out to them that there are other values they ought not to violate are not likely to be heeded. But in any case it is at least essential that when something goes wrong in a community relationship, one who would seek to set it right proceed on the assumption that the other members of the community are acting with good will. Starting with the opposite assumption—of ill will—undercuts the very possibility of community from the start.

Furthermore, in some cases it may be better to maintain an imperfect community—such as the sort of unhappy but tolerable family situation described above—than to transform the entire relationship into a contractual one. A community, even an imperfect one, at least contains the seeds of growth in personal relationship, but a contract is in itself impersonal.

Between those who do violence and those who have violence done to them there can never be community—at least not while the violence is occurring. Community depends on mutual self-commitment, and there is no sharing among people who do violence to one another. True, it may be justifiable to resort to violence in some complex communities: for example, to overthrow an oppressive dictator (whose *de facto* government may have, in extreme cases, a relationship to the governed not dissimilar to that of an armed mob to an unarmed populace which it is terrorizing). In such cases those who employ violence are clearly not maintaining community with the individual or group against whom the violence is directed, but it may be that the use of violence is in fact the only way of preserving the possibility of community for everyone else.

Such cases are, however, rare. And, other things being equal, the larger the group to whom violence is done, the less likely it is that the violence is justifiable, at least as an instrument of preserving community.

As a practical matter, this suggests that the smaller the number of revolutionaries in a given society in relation to the society as a whole, the better are the chances that the revolutionaries are themselves would-be tyrants, obsessed perhaps by some scheme for transforming human nature by means which will turn out to be violent and exploitative in their turn. Whatever their rhetoric may assert, such people do not really have community in view; instead they are bent on imposing on everyone else their vision of how people should live and how society should function.

Social change brought about by violence will be no more stable than the ability of those who employed the violence to remain in power. As long as they have not received the consent of those they govern, they are only exercising a kind of tyranny. At best such a situation may represent a kind of contractual relationship; it can in particular cases be an improvement over a previously existing situation of exploitation. But it is far removed from community, and it may retard rather than advance the attainment of a truly communitarian relationship among persons.

Questions for Review and Discussion

1. To what extent, do you think, do the ills of society arise from moral evil and to what extent from other causes?

2. In practice, how are the exploitative, contractual, and communitarian aspects of a society to be distinguished, when in fact they are mixed in the same social situation?

3. Can you think of historical cases in which a nonideological rebellion of a genuinely exploited group of people succeeded in changing the situation of exploitation? How did the exploiters come to miscalculate?

4. We speak of a contractual relationship as midway between exploitation and community. This is an oversimplified, shorthand way of putting the matter. Can you think of more nuanced ways of defining the similarities and the differences of the various forms of relationship?

5. It has been said that in the United States there is a tendency for every great social issue sooner or later to come before the Supreme Court. Can you explain why this is so in terms of the analysis offered in this chapter?

6. Existing ways of treating criminals apparently tend, at least in many cases, to alienate them still further from society. But some proposals for reform are based on an at least implicit denial of freedom of self-determination. Assuming freedom of self-determination, is there any way to deal with a criminal which would be better than present methods?

7. In this chapter we take a rather dim view of revolution, especially revolution on ideological grounds. Does this mean that our position is committed to a conservative or status quo stance on issues involving social justice?

8. For lack of space the brief treatment offered here does not go into a number of important questions, such as civil disobedience. Investigate what is involved in civil disobedience and other tactics of confrontation politics and discuss the extent to which such activities might be justified and under what conditions.

9. To what extent is the present discussion applicable to the relations between nations? Is permanent peace possible, or is war inevitable?

① Hinders people from doing what is ethically right.
② On ethical grounds religion destroys human freedom.
③ Evil & Religion

19: The Role of Religion

Is religion a help or a hindrance to morality?

The question sounds odd. Religion and morality are often equated, so that a religious person is assumed to be a moral person. Only slightly more sophisticated is the attitude which looks on religion as an indispensable—or at least extremely helpful—bulwark of morality. How many tributes have been paid to "religion, the foundation of good citizenship and good conduct"? But the relationship between religion and morality is not that simple.

For one thing, there plainly is no necessary connection between religious belief and morally good behavior. People who hold very strong religious beliefs can commit moral atrocities. People with no visible or identifiable religious convictions can lead morally exemplary lives. As we shall see, religious commitment can indeed provide strong support for ethically correct behavior; but there is no necessary connection between the two things. Being good and being religious are separate and distinct.

Furthermore, as we remarked earlier, the effort to tie religion to morality can have unfortunate results: specifically, the result of making religion the handmaid of ethics. In its most simplistic form this comes down to reducing religion to a single formula: "Be good or you won't go to heaven."

It may be true that being good (trying to do what one

199

regards as morally right) is a precondition to going to heaven (achieving a permanently satisfactory relationship with the transcendent Other whom we call God), although whether it is or is not is beyond the scope of this discussion. But the difficulty with the formulation is that it debases both salvation and goodness by making one the payoff for the other. In this way of looking at things religion and moral goodness are placed in the context of second-level, means-end action, rather than third-level action: action performed for the sake of a basic good in which one participates precisely in performing the action.

At this point it is perhaps necessary to state something both obvious and important. In using words like "God," "religion," "heaven," "salvation," and so forth we are not now departing from our established procedure and taking for granted the truth of religion in general or the Christian religion in particular. We are not taking it for granted that there is a God or that heaven exists, nor do we propose to demonstrate the existence of either.

Instead, we merely assume that many of our readers do in fact hold religious convictions and will therefore be interested in considering how ethics relates to such beliefs. Our purpose is to examine this question: How do—or should—religion and the subject matter of ethics relate to each other? One need not assume the truth of religion in order to discuss the question.

1. Objections to Religion

If the relationship of religion to ethics is not as cut-and-dried as many people believe, for others it is not apparent at all or at least it is not apparent that there is any positive relationship. On the contrary, many objections are raised to religion on ethical grounds. In different ways these say the same thing: Not only does religion not necessarily foster good behavior, but it actually hinders people in their efforts to do what is ethically right. Such objections generally take one of three forms.

First, it is said that by focusing attention on the transcendent—on God, salvation, heaven, the afterlife, and such—religion distracts human beings from the here and now and causes them to neglect their responsibilities in and to the world and the people around them. This is the argument against supernatural religion advanced by John Dewey and by Karl Marx ("Religion is the opiate of the people"). Holding out the promise of happiness in a future life, religion seduces human beings from the task of correcting evils and injustices in this life.

It is nearly inevitable that religion should be open to this charge. As was suggested above, there is for practical purposes no way to motivate children—or people who, while beyond childhood, are still morally immature—except by promising them a reward for acting in a certain way. In a religious context this naturally leads to the formulation: "Be good or you won't go to heaven." And it seems clear that some popular expressions of religion have tended to batten onto this formula almost to the exclusion of any other consideration.

Nevertheless, a true religious act is a third-level action: an act performed not simply to achieve a specific future objective (heaven, eternal life) but in order to participate in the good of religion now. A pattern of acts of this sort can be described as "living a holy life."

Notice that when one refers to persons as "living holy lives," one is speaking of them as doing something here and now. Their action represents present participation in a good: in this case the good of religion. So one might speak of other persons as "living scholarly lives" (participating consistently in the good of truth or knowledge) or "living a sociable life" (participating consistently in the good of friendship).

Such expressions describe the pattern of life of people who

are not acting merely in order to achieve specific objectives but are instead participating in certain goods. Nor are such individuals necessarily highly sophisticated persons who speak of "third-level action" and such and have a well worked-out theory of human behavior and ethics. What is in question here are people's fundamental attitudes and commitments, not their command of ethical theory. In any case, whatever else one might say of persons who live holy lives (that is, participate consistently in the good of religion), one cannot accuse them of ignoring the here and now. They are participating here and now in the good of religion, and doing so to such an extent that their manner of living can be characterized by the expression "living holy lives."

It may be objected that this still leaves such people open to the accusation of ignoring other human goods. If, however, they are really doing what they are said to do—participating consistently in the good of religion—this cannot be the case. As we have seen earlier, the four basic goods—which we have called for convenience's sake integrity, authenticity, friendship, and religion, and which we grouped under the general heading of "reflexive" purposes—are mutually dependent, so that to the extent one acts contrary to one of them, one undermines one's participation in all. Stated positively, this means that a person committed to and participating in one fundamental reflexive human good, such as the good of religion, will also act, so far as he or she can, to realize the other reflexive human goods.

Furthermore, just as a basic commitment to one good—truth or friendship, for instance—does no more than constitute the framework within which individuals will work out their particular relationships to all the goods, so people whose basic commitment is to the good of religion have merely established the emphasis and orientation of their lives, according to which they will seek to work out their relationship to all the other goods besides religion. People who are really living holy lives have not cut themselves off from everything else in human life except religion, any more than people who are leading scholarly lives have cut themselves off from everything else except knowledge; they have only established for themselves the terms according to which everything else will be fitted into their lives and they will relate to everything else.

2. Religion and Freedom

A second objection advanced against religion on ethical grounds is that it destroys human freedom. According to religion, it is said, human beings are good if they are obedient to God's will; but to make goodness contingent on obedience to God is to withdraw from human beings their autonomy and reduce them to a state of subjection. This complaint is found in the work of a number of writers, notably Nietzsche, for whom it is a major theme.

Like the first objection to religion, this one also has a kind of inevitability about it, given the need to present religious claims to children and others who are morally immature. For such persons it is virtually inescapable that religious purposes and imperatives be presented as a system of rules to which obedience is demanded. Yet at the same time there does exist in this an obvious danger: the danger of suggesting that the gulf between God and human beings is of the same sort as that between the exploiter and the exploited.

One solution—a false one—lies in asserting that religion makes no demands on anyone: religion has no connection with morality, is in fact fundamentally amoral. But it is difficult to see how such religion could contribute anything to achieving reconciliation, which all religious systems posit as necessary and desirable, between human beings and the transcendent. If there is a need for reconciliation, something must be *done* to bring it about. This implies acting in certain ways, not acting in others.

A better solution to the objection is found in the fact that, as we have seen, responsibilities are not imposed externally but instead arise naturally from reality—the reality of the human person. Persons are not morally responsible because God arbitrarily requires them to observe a merely external set of rules. Rather, people have a responsibility to respect and seek to participate in human goods because it is humanly right and good to do so. People who act morally—as we have explained what it means to act morally—achieve fuller realization of their personhood by doing so: their humanity is enhanced, not debased. Since acting morally essentially means acting within the framework of a fundamental commitment or coherent set of commitments, one might well speak of people who act in this way as acting with committed freedom, the freedom of self-determination. The contrary state of affairs—acting on the basis of *un*committed freedom— suggests either a merely premoral or amoral spontaneity or a "doing what one pleases" which is immoral.

Furthermore, even assuming a religious duty to do what God wills, the responsibilities associated with religion become moral responsibilities in precisely the same way as the moral responsibilities which arise from any other basic human good. That is, the very moral responsibilities which arise from the good of religion are binding in the same way and for the same general reasons as the responsibilities which arise from the goods of truth and friendship: one has the responsibility of doing some things and not doing others because that is how one realizes more fully what it means to be human. If there is a God who commands us to do things, his commands are to be obeyed because what is commanded is humanly—in the deepest meaning of that word—right and good; it is simply not the case that what is commanded becomes right and good from the fact that God commands it, in the sense of imposing it externally on us.

3. Religion and Evil

A third ethical objection to religion is based on the fact of evil. God cannot be both good and powerful, or else he would not permit evil to exist. Some religious theories have attempted to answer this objection by speculating that God is in fact not powerful enough to prevent evil; the principle of good and the principle of evil, it is suggested, are more or less coequal, and the struggle between them results in victory sometimes for one, sometimes for the other.

A better solution emerges when one realizes that "good" has many different meanings, and there is no logical reason to suppose that our human understanding of what is good necessarily applies unequivocally to the transcendent being whom we call God. It is unreasonable to attempt to measure divine action or nonaction according to the norms of human moral goodness. In an earlier edition of this book we suggested, by way of example, that God could hypothetically be a utilitarian—because, presumably, an all-knowing being would possess the common denominator of goodness which is not accessible to human intelligence. While it now seems to us that this is a misleading formulation, even as a speculation, and easily subject to misinterpretation, it at least suggests the essential point we wish to make: that it is unreasonable to try to apply simplistically a morality based on human goods to a being who is, by definition, nonhuman. One ought rather to take it for granted that what it means for God to be good will be radically different from what it means for a human being to be good.

A variation on this objection is the assertion that religion itself has been and remains a force for evil in human affairs.

Religion is an outlet for fanaticism, an occasion and excuse
for people to act cruelly and unjustly toward others. This
accusation has been leveled against religion by such writers as
Voltaire, David Hume, and, in our own day, Bertrand Russell.

Its impact comes from the fact that it is true, although it is
not the whole truth. A person can indeed practice fanaticism
in the name of religion, since an exclusive (and exclusivistic)
concentration on one category of human good at the expense
of others is precisely what is meant by fanaticism. As there are
fanatics in the pursuit of knowledge, fanatics in the pursuit of
sensuality, fanatics in the pursuit of the whole range of
human experiences, so, too, there are fanatics in the pursuit
of religion.

There is no necessary reason, however, why religion
should tend to breed fanaticism. Those who suggest otherwise mistake an abuse of religion for its whole reality. It is
entirely possible to give the central place in one's life to the
human good of religion without making that particular good
an absolute to which all else must be sacrificed. The good of
religion is, after all, not identical with God, and even in traditional religious terms the quest for union with God is seen
as involving an effort to respect and participate in many different goods besides those in the category of religion.

In the Christian tradition—which we cite here only by way
of example—even Jesus, who according to orthodox faith is
believed to be God made man, acted as a human being according to the conditions of human good. And the individual
Christian, it is further believed, must conform to God by conformity to Jesus in his human nature. Christianity proposes,
in other words, that people respond to the call to share intimately in divine life not by evading human responsibility, not
by living inhumanly, but by fulfilling the requirements of
what it means to be human. Christianity thus demands of its
adherents that they be open to the fullness of human person-

hood, not that they be limited to the fanatical pursuit of one aspect or another of that personhood.

4. Religion and Hope

There is more to be said about the relationship between ethics and religion than simply responding to ethical objections to religion. For there is, or can be, a positive relationship between the two, a relationship in which religion supports the individual in the effort to live a morally good life. To say this is not to assume the truth of religion, but only to point to the fact that hope, founded on traditional religious beliefs and attitudes, does strongly buttress the effort of many people to do what is ethically right.

The key word here is hope. And hope relates directly to the fact of evil.

Faced with the fact of evil in the world, one is tempted to respond in either of two ways: with a kind of technological-humanistic presumption which takes for granted that if only the proper techniques are found and applied, evil will be eradicated from human life, or with a despair which takes for granted that evil is ineradicable and can never be fully overcome. The former attitude is illustrated by theories of progress and perfectibility which deny freedom of self-determination—the sort of theories so prevalent in our Western culture which we have criticized repeatedly. The latter attitude is illustrated by theories of fatalism and rejection of the reality of the world, which also deny freedom of self-determination; these theories have been prevalent in Eastern cultures. Hope—a hope founded in religion—makes it possible to avoid both extremes.

Hope in this sense comes down to the conviction that doing what is right will not be fundamentally at odds with human well-being, even when doing what is right means refusing to do something which, though wrong, nevertheless seems to have humanly good consequences. This is of crucial importance, for it is clear that doing what is right often has painful consequences and that, on the contrary, there are frequently cases in which, humanly speaking and up to a point, immorality does pay.

Hope founded on religious belief enables us to cope with these facts and, in coping, to continue to do what is morally right. It does this by making it possible for us to hold as a rational belief the conviction that evil will ultimately be overcome, even though we cannot say how or when.

Only if one has such hope can one readily reject a morality of consequences, which holds that it is right to do evil so that good will come about. With such hope it is possible to say in effect, "Even though I do not see the good consequences of doing what is morally right in this difficult case, I will nevertheless do it, convinced that my responsibility as a free person is to do what is humanly good—to respect all of the human goods—not to achieve all human good consequences."

Religion in this sense is hardly a solution to the human moral predicament. It is not a panacea for the problem of evil, any more than psychoanalysis or social revolution or some theory of education is a panacea for this profound problem. If religion or anything else is regarded as a panacea, the result will be frustration. We are not suggesting that religion is a solution for evil; instead, we are pointing out that religion can be, has been, and still is a support for many people in their efforts to do what is right in the face of evil.

Religion does no more and no less than place the paradox of moral evil in a perspective in which it is possible to live with it, neither rebelling nor despairing. To say that one can live with evil does not mean that one regards it complacently or fails to do what one can, consistent with the requirements of ethically good behavior, to correct and remove it. It means that one recognizes that because human beings are free, moral evil is and will continue to be a reality in human life; but, in the context of religious belief, it means further that one remains convinced that evil will ultimately be overcome, although we do not know how this will come about.

Finally, speaking now as persons who hold the Christian faith, we shall add one further thought. Although Jesus is a divine person, he willingly accepted the responsibilities of human freedom and thus demonstrated that this freedom is compatible with divine personhood. The implications for the individual Christian are enormous. Christianity not only allows but demands that people approach the challenge of living with the intention of realizing as fully as they can all that it truly means to be human. Christianity need not stunt or degrade persons; on the contrary, Christianity, understood as it really is, teaches humankind to respect the dignity of the human person and all that constitutes a person. And, finally, Christianity teaches that with God's help human freedom will be able to fulfill the responsibilities which freedom entails.

Questions for Review and Discussion

1. To what extent, do you think, has religion, as a matter of historical fact, distracted people from the here-and-now goods of this life?

2. Can you think of historical figures or people you know who you would say were really living holy lives and at the same time were committed to realizing human goods here and now?

3. Various types of religion have used various substantive goods as their vehicles. Show how life, aesthetic experience, play, and speculative knowledge have been vehicles for religion in various forms of it.

4. Can you think of examples in which substantive goods, serving as vehicles for religion, have been perverted to the status of mere means? Does the same thing also happen when other reflexive goods become the objects of strong commitment?

5. Can you think of any reason why religion especially should give rise to fanaticism?

6. It has been said that the difference between martyrs and fanatics is that martyrs are willing to die for what they believe in while fanatics are willing to kill for what they believe in. Discuss.

7. Relate Augustine's conception of happiness, discussed in chapter three, to the fear, discussed in the present chapter, that religion infringes on human freedom.

8. Why do most people assume that God should act in a morally good way according to human standards of morality?

9. What is the difference between hope and optimism?

10. Do you agree that there is a relationship between religious conviction and the ability to resist utilitarianism? If so, do you think the relationship is the one sketched out here, or is there more to it than that?

20: We Must Decide
Who We Shall Be

Many possible life-styles are good. All of us must choose among them for ourselves. The choice is one which no one else can make for us.

Indeed, we must all make many important decisions which profoundly shape our lives: whether or not to marry—and whom; what our occupation will be; where we shall live. It is true that such decisions are influenced and limited by circumstances over which we have no control. But it is also true that for a normal individual in normal circumstances such decisions do bring into play freedom of self-determination.

These basic, life-determining choices concern the goods to which we shall join with others in order to make our personal contribution to the common task of humankind. No one can set down hard-and-fast rules for making these basic decisions. But it is possible to offer some general suggestions.

To begin with, if we are to choose wisely, we should try to know ourselves as well as we can. This means discovering our capacities and special talents, and also recognizing and accepting our limitations. That does not imply committing oneself only to sure things—to small, limited goals which can be easily achieved. But it does require that we commit ourselves to purposes which we have a reasonable chance of realizing.

It would be unreasonable for a person who lacked the basic requirements of temperament and inclination to aspire, even in the name of some higher good, to be a contemplative hermit. But it would be unworthy of a person probably endowed with the gifts of a concert pianist to settle down to a more certain career in an unchallenging line of work. High aspirations in the framework of a realistic assessment of oneself are the key.

1. The Myth of the Well-rounded Person

Although no one can really do everything well, our culture sometimes pressures us to make the attempt. One enduring myth about self-determination and human development concerns the ideal of the well-rounded person: the individual who is developed in all aspects.

This notion has its uses if it is not carried too far: if it means only that a person should not become so wrapped up in one area of endeavor as completely to neglect other matters to which he or she ought to give attention (e.g., the job-oriented person who has no time to spare for sociability, recreation, or even intimacy with his or her family). But the myth of the well-rounded person becomes a pernicious thing when it involves people expending tremendous amounts of time and energy in the attempt to do a bit of everything—an attempt whose usual result is that nothing is done really well.

Generous and altruistic people make this sort of mistake at least as easily as anyone else, and perhaps more readily than most. The classic do-gooder is into every cause and campaign, from human rights to "no nukes," and often fails to make a significant contribution to any. Granted that there are many good causes in the world—many situations of evil and injustice which require redress—this does not mean that every person should become extensively involved in crusading on behalf of them all. We must make choices; we must opt for certain areas of concentration in preference to others; and doing so is not only not bad but positively good if it makes it possible for us to do well something which is worth doing.

2. Making Basic Commitments

We should try to know as well as we can what possibilities are really open to us before choosing one or another. It too often happens that even intelligent and well-educated people drift into extremely important commitments without making a careful investigation of the alternatives and without consulting others who could help them deliberate wisely.

A conspicuous example is the careless way in which many people enter marriage, only to regret the decision as soon as the honeymoon is over, if not before. It is no disparagement of romantic love, merely a recognition of its limitations as a basis for making sound choices, to say that two responsible people considering marriage will base their decision on other grounds in addition to the way they happen to feel about each other at the moment.

Having assessed our abilities and also the possibilities which are open to us, we should try to match our particular abilities to the possibilities we perceive. In doing so we should be quite deliberate and cautious (not the same thing, incidentally, as being merely timid and indecisive). In matters of fundamental importance one should never proceed simply on the basis of the information which happens to be immediately available. We should reflect on ourselves and on the situation rather than simply follow the bidding of imagination and feeling.

At the same time, though, we should take our feelings into account in this process of reflection, conscious that feelings often mirror something important about our deeper selves. Usually we make a mistake if we try to force ourselves into a commitment contrary to our strong feelings. It is hard to be very optimistic about the prospects of a young man who has had to force himself to become a doctor or a young woman who has had to struggle against her emotions to bring herself to the point of saying "Yes" to a suitor.

Still, in the making of commitments one should not be so excessively cautious as to make only safe choices and opt only for things which carry a "can't miss" label. Indeed, one must be willing to risk failure and the pain of failure, realizing that success—achieving what one has set out to do—is not essential to the morally good life and that failure by itself is not morally wrong.

Many good and important things have been accomplished only because some person or persons were willing to risk failure. (Just as, of course, many people who have accepted this risk have actually failed—not indeed morally but in a practical sense.) From the point of view of ethics it is not success or failure that determines goodness; it is commitment or lack of commitment to the realization of human goods, and action or lack of action to carry out this commitment.

3. How Many Commitments?

One should not make too many commitments. This does not mean hanging back and refusing to extend oneself: there is nothing morally good about such an attitude. But it is also important to realize that every serious commitment carries with it serious moral responsibilities, which often involve others besides ourselves. It is neither prudent nor good to take on so many such responsibilities that one is simply unable, for want of time or strength or talent, to satisfy them all and therefore must either neglect all of them to some degree or some of them entirely.

At the same time we should not fall into the trap of supposing that by accepting commitments we are somehow limiting our freedom—a notion put forward by Sartre. A freedom without content, which was in effect no more than a vague and unspecified openness to every sort of experience and activity without commitment to any, would be meaningless. We have spoken before of committed freedom: people shape their lives and their selves by the commitments they freely undertake. Refusal to make commitments is refusal to live as a person.

The responsibility which we all have to constitute our lives—our selves—is our own and no one else's. It is a serious mistake to allow this fundamental matter to be settled by the expectations, however benign, of others—parents, relatives, friends, the communities to which we belong, public opinion. We should listen to the counsel of others, but we must not let others make our fundamental decisions for us.

Altogether too many people, consciously or unconsciously, do in fact fulfill roles which have been predesigned for them by others. The process by which this happens can be quite subtle, and considerable vigilance may be required to prevent its happening. At present, popular culture vehemently attacks role-playing, but that same culture simultaneously exerts powerful influences on individuals to conform to its standards and fit themselves to the roles which it happens to approve. In such circumstances the potential for being victimized unawares is very great.

In order to pull together the strands of our lives and be unified persons, we must all make some most basic commitment which is broad enough to embrace all of our other commitments. Like a theme running through a piece of music, such a fundamental commitment gives coherence and pattern to what would otherwise be the disordered fragments of life.

If this commitment is to be made inclusivistically, it cannot be to one of the substantive goods—life, play, aesthetic experience, speculative knowledge—or to some part or aspect of these, because these goods cannot be realized in every act of our lives. Thus, the most basic, unifying commitment must be to one of the reflexive goods—integrity, authenticity, friendship, religion—which are intrinsically connected, so that it is impossible to participate fully in any one of them without also being open to and participating in the others.

Even so, it is possible and indeed necessary that the emphasis of a person's most basic commitment be more on one of these goods than on the others. The others are not excluded; they simply take on a specific meaning—a special coloration, one might say—from the good to which the primary emphasis is given.

On which of these goods should an individual place the emphasis of his or her life? It seems doubtful to us that an absolutely definitive philosophical argument can be made in favor of one rather than the others. At the same time it also seems clear that for a person who is already a religious believer religion quite reasonably will play this unifying role. Once again, we must emphasize that we are not attempting to introduce apologetics under the guise of philosophy; we are merely remarking that a Christian, a Jew, or an adherent of some other religion will appropriately place the unifying emphasis of his or her life upon the good of religion. In doing so such a person will create a congenial framework for realization of the other goods—for seeking harmony within the self (integrity) and between the self and one's action (authenticity), and for pursuing a correct relationship between oneself and other people (friendship and justice), all in the context of establishing and maintaining a satisfactory relationship with the transcendent Other whom we call God.

To the extent that we identify the transcendent Other with the principle which sustains human goods, even when they are not chosen, making one's religious commitment most fundamental is closely related to—if not identical with—taking one's moral stand on the side of openness to all of the human goods. Emphasis upon this good can fulfill the need for integration of the person, without in any way constricting or devaluating one's proper concern for harmony within one's self and with one's neighbor.

We have come, then, to the end of this discussion, and we find that we are in a sense back at the point from which we began. The fundamental responsibility of human freedom is the responsibility faced by all of us to create our own lives, our own selves, through the choices we make. We can use this freedom well or badly, but we cannot avoid using it. Using freedom well means choosing in ways which progressively open us to ever-greater realization of what it means to be human persons; using freedom badly means choosing in ways which limit and eventually kill our capacity for further growth.

Ethics, far from being a stereotyped set of do's and don'ts, is an effort on the part of human reason to provide guidelines for making choices which make possible our continued growth as human persons. Only when we choose in this way and continue to grow as persons can we truly be fulfilled.

Such fulfillment is not the same as gratification or practical success. To live in a morally good way is always more or less difficult, almost inevitably involves us in pain, and may enmesh us in tragedy, if by tragedy one means failure to achieve limited goals and objectives. This, however, is the reality and the dignity of human life. Freedom is both blessing and burden. In both aspects it lies at the heart of what it means to be human.

Questions for Review and Discussion

1. Does the view that there are many different life-styles from which to choose admit an element of subjectivism or relativism into this ethics?

2. Why may good people not be conformists?

3. Why do you think the ideal of the well-rounded person has such a strong hold on the thinking of many people?

4. Should counseling help people avoid drifting into important commitments without sufficient consideration? Has it done so for you or for people whom you know?

5. To what extent do you take your feelings into account when making important decisions? Of all the emotions which one or ones do you think it most important to pay attention to?

6. Do you think your friends and acquaintances are sufficiently willing to risk failure in life, or are they more likely to settle for greater security for themselves rather than run risks for important human goods?

7. Some people make basic commitments in life mainly due to adolescent rebellion. For instance, they get married because their parents are against it. Others make their basic commitments too much under the influence of others: for example, by entering a certain profession because their parents have always counted on this for them. What signs would characterize a commitment which is really personal and which is not unduly influenced in either of these directions?

8. Do you agree that it is necessary to have some overarching commitment which organizes and harmonizes all the other basic commitments of one's life? If so, do you think we are correct in suggesting that, at least for religious believers, it is very appropriate that this should be a commitment to the religious purpose? Is it possible for good people to integrate their lives in some other way?

Suggestions for Further Reading and Research

These suggestions are not intended as a general bibliography for the field of ethics. Many of the topics we treat are discussed in articles in the *Encyclopedia of Philosophy;* these articles usually introduce various positions on a topic and provide rather extensive bibliography. R. B. Brandt, *Ethical Theories: The Problems of Normative and Critical Ethics* (Englewood Cliffs, N.J.: Prentice-Hall, 1959), summarizes and criticizes many ethical theories and provides very good bibliographies. W. T. Jones, Frederick Sontag, M. O. Beckner, and R. J. Fogelin, eds., *Approaches to Ethics,* 2nd ed. (New York: McGraw-Hill, 1969) is a good collection of selections from major philosophic works in ethics from Plato to the present. Vernon J. Bourke, *History of Ethics* (Garden City, N.Y.: Doubleday, 1968), is an excellent, up-to-date history of ethics; this work is also available (1970) in two paperback volumes. T. E. Hill, *Contemporary Ethical Theories* (New York: Macmillan, 1951), briefly treats almost all current theories.

Philip B. Rice, *Our Knowledge of Good and Evil* (New York: Random House, 1955), includes a useful summary and critique of the many positions developed in Anglo-American ethics from about 1900–1950. Henry B. Veatch, *For an Ontology of Morals: A Critique of Contemporary Ethical Theory* (Evanston: Northwestern U. Press, 1971), systematically criticizes contemporary theories and points in the direction of an ethics something like ours; Veatch's book could be a useful introduction to ours for the more advanced reader.

Our discussion of freedom in chapter one owes much to, but freely departs from, Mortimer J. Adler, *The Idea of Freedom: A Dialectical Examination of the Conception of Freedom*, 2 vols. (Garden City, N.Y.: Doubleday, 1958 and 1961). Joseph M. Boyle, Jr., Germain Grisez, and Olaf Tollefsen, *Free Choice: A Self-Referential Argument* (Notre Dame and London: University of Notre Dame Press, 1976), greatly expands the treatment given here and describes all the main arguments for and against free choice. Austin Farrer, *The Freedom of the Will* (London: Adam & Charles Block, 1958), esp. pp. 132–139, develops the point that in practice one must think and act on the supposition of freedom.

Hannah Arendt, *The Human Condition* (Chicago and London: U. of Chicago Press, 1958), pp. 79–247, distinguishes labor, work, and action—roughly corresponding to our first-, second-, and third-level action. Gabriel Marcel, *Being and Having: An Existential Diary* (New York: Harper & Row, 1965), pp. 154–174, distinguishes being and having—roughly corresponding to our third and second levels of action, respectively. Aristotle, *Nichomachean Ethics,* book 6, distinguishes between art and prudence—roughly corresponding to our second and third levels of action, respectively. John Dewey, *Reconstruction in Philosophy* (Boston: Beacon, 1957), pp. 161–170, presents a version of situation ethics. Joseph Fletcher, *Situation Ethics: The New Morality* (Philadelphia: Westminster, 1966), pp. 26–31, 134–145, treats the situation as determinant of morality.

Mortimer J. Adler, *The Time of Our Lives: The Ethics of Common Sense* (New York: Holt, Rinehart, and Winston, 1970), pp. 3–63, sees the ethical problem as one of giving meaning to life; he does not distinguish second- and third-level action sharply but does (pp. 86–97) explain that neither pleasure nor a technical end can give meaning to life. Robert Nozick, *Anar-*

chy, State, and Utopia (New York: Basic Books, Inc., 1974), pp. 42–45, argues against equating pleasure with fulfillment much as we do; although his book ultimately defends positions with which we do not agree, it contains many clever arguments and useful clarifications. St. Augustine, *City of God*, book 19, presents the classic doctrine of heaven as principle of meaning for human life. Germain G. Grisez, "Man, the Natural End of," *New Catholic Encyclopedia*, vol. 9, pp. 132–138, criticizes traditional conceptions of man's natural end. Vatican Council II, *The Church in the Modern World*, part 1, chap. 3, moderates the Augustinian emphasis on heaven as future as it stresses that the kingdom of God is already present in mystery.

Our references to Aristotle in chapter four are to *Nichomachean Ethics*, books 1 and 10. Henry B. Veatch, *Rational Man: A Modern Interpretation of Aristotelian Ethics* (Bloomington: Indiana U. Press, 1964), pp. 148–154, introduces freedom, which alters Aristotle's position in the direction of ours. Gabriel Marcel, *Creative Fidelity*, trans. Robert Rosthal (New York: Farrar, Straus, 1964), pp. 104–119, presents the life of a person as a unique act. Charles Fried, *An Anatomy of Values: Problems of Personal and Social Choice* (Cambridge, Mass.: Harvard U. Press, 1970), pp. 87–101, introduces the concept of "life plan" and considers life as an ordered set of rational acts. John Rawls, *A Theory of Justice* (Cambridge, Mass.: Harvard U. Press, 1971), pp. 551–567, argues against hedonism and against any theory that tries to reduce the human good to a single good.

Our treatment of community in chapter five owes much to, but freely departs from, Aristotle, *Nichomachean Ethics*, book five (justice) and books eight and nine (friendship); the distinction between friendship of utility and friendship based on virtue corresponds to our distinction between contract and community. Charles Fried, *An Anatomy of Values*, pp. 105–115, outlines a concept of society similar to our idea of community.

Yves R. Simon, *Philosophy of Democratic Government* (Chicago and London: U. of Chicago Press, 1951), deals with democratic society as a potential form of community; Simon is especially helpful for his treatment of the problem of authority (see his *A General Theory of Authority* [1962; reprint ed., Notre Dame: U. of Notre Dame Press, 1980]).

A classic statement of the subjectivism we discuss in chapter six is Bertrand Russell, *Human Society in Ethics and Politics* (London: Allen & Unwin; New York: Simon & Schuster, 1955). A good example of relativism is W. G. Sumner, *Folkways* (Boston: Ginn, 1934). J. D. Mabbott, *An Introduction to Ethics* (Garden City, N.Y.: Doubleday, 1969), pp. 70–102, criticizes subjectivism. Peter A. Bertocci and Richard M. Millard, *Personality and the Good: Psychological and Ethical Perspectives* (New York: David McKay, 1963), pp. 260–294, criticize relativism and subjectivism. Vernon J. Bourke, *Ethics in Crisis* (Milwaukee: Bruce, 1966), pp. 102–119, takes up the problem of objective values in light of recent work in anthropology. Morris Ginsberg, *On the Diversity of Morals* (London: Mercury Books, 1962), pp. 26–40, 97–129, criticizes cultural relativism. Abraham Edel, *Ethical Judgment: The Use of Science in Ethics* (Glencoe, Ill.: Free Press, 1955), criticizes relativism; out of this develops the concept of a "valuational base" (pp. 297–310), the content of which is what we attempt to formulate in chapter seven.

Also relevant to chapter seven is a tentative analysis of human needs by Bertocci and Millard, *Personality and the Good*, pp. 157–172. A. H. Maslow, *Motivation and Personality* (New York: Harper & Row, 1954), pp. 80–106, gives a psychologist's approach to basic needs roughly corresponding to our fundamental purposes. William K. Frankena, *Ethics*, 2nd ed. (Englewood Cliffs, N.J.: Prentice-Hall, 1973), p. 88, gives a list similar to but longer than our list of intrinsic goods.

Erich Fromm, *Man for Himself* (New York: Rinehart, 1947), presents a theory of human goodness which reduces it to health. Thomas Aquinas, *Truth*, vol. 3, trans. R. W. Schmidt (Chicago: Henry Regnery, 1954), question 21, presents a tight treatise on good, which really amounts to an entire value theory. Germain Grisez, "The First Principle of Practical Reason: A Commentary on the *Summa theologiae*, 1-2, question 94, article 2," *Natural Law Forum*, vol. 10 (1965), pp. 168-201, a technical expression of our value theory, with some critique of alternatives.

Chapter nine's treatment of the basic principle of morality has few parallels in other literature. Among the few are Rudolf Allers, *The Psychology of Character*, trans. E. B. Strauss (London and New York: Sheed & Ward, 1933), pp. 206-240, which represents "true and false ideals" of character corresponding to our distinction, but in psychological terms. Joseph de Finance, S. J., *Essai sur l'agir humain* (Rome: Université Grégorienne, 1962), pp. 304-348, locates moral value in the openness of free commitment to the transcendent, moral disvalue in closedness upon a particular value.

The utilitarianism discussed in chapter ten received a classic formulation in Jeremy Bentham, *An Introduction to the Principles of Morals and Legislation* (New York: Hefner, 1948), pp. 1-42. Also John Stuart Mill, *Utilitarianism* (New York: Library of the Liberal Arts, 1954). John Dewey develops his situationism in *Reconstruction in Philosophy*, pp. 161-170. Joseph Fletcher's *Situation Ethics* is his fullest expression of his theory; Fletcher was criticized very effectively by Paul Ramsey, *Deeds and Rules in Christian Ethics* (New York: Charles Scribners' Sons, 1967), pp. 145-225. A book-length critique of utilitarianism is David Lyons, *Forms and Limits of Utilitarianism* (Oxford: Clarendon Press, 1965). A brief critique of utilitarianism and outline of the present theory: Germain Grisez, "Methods of Ethical Inquiry," *Proceedings of the American Catholic Philosophical Association*, vol. 41 (1967), pp. 160-168. For a much more developed critique of utilitarianism and every form of consequentialism see Germain Grisez, "Against Consequentialism," *American Journal of Jurisprudence,* 23 (1978), pp. 21–72.

Many works could be cited to illustrate the philosophic development of one or another of the modes of responsibility in chapter eleven. John Rawls, *A Theory of Justice,* pp. 407–433 (and see works referred to p. 408) presents a position similar to the first mode of responsibility. R. M. Hare, *Freedom and Reason* (New York: Oxford U. Press, 1965), builds his ethics on the second mode of responsibility, which had its classic treatment in Immanuel Kant, *Foundations of the Metaphysics of Morals,* trans. Lewis White Beck (Indianapolis: Library of Liberal Arts, 1959), p. 50, and *passim.* For a critique of Hare and a contrast of his view with that of St. Thomas see Joseph M. Boyle, Jr., "Aquinas and Prescriptive Ethics," *Proceedings of the American Catholic Philosophical Association,* 49 (1975), pp. 82–95. An ancient work, Epictetus, *Discourses,* bases ethics on the fourth mode of responsibility. Josiah Royce, *The Philosophy of Loyalty* (New York: Macmillan, 1908), develops an admirable balance of the fourth and fifth modes; he also has a good understanding of the idea of commitment, and his thinking is not far from the idea of openness to all goods as a criterion of morality. Gabriel Marcel, *Creative Fidelity* (previously cited), pp. 147–174, deals with the fifth mode.

Chapter twelve's treatment of duties can be supplemented by close study of Aristotle, *Nichomachean Ethics,* book 5 (justice). An ethics of duty is F. H. Bradley, *Ethical Studies* (Indianapolis: Library of Liberal Arts, 1951), esp. pp. 98–112. Current points of view are represented in J. A. Bedau, ed., *Justice and Equality* (Englewood Cliffs, N.J.: Prentice-Hall, 1971).

Chapter thirteen's treatment of the eighth mode of responsibility will be illustrated in the concise traditional statement of Thomas Aquinas, *Summa theologiae,* 1–2, question 20, article 2. Eric d'Arcy, *Human Acts: An Essay in Their Moral Evaluation* (Oxford: Clarendon Press, 1963), does not go as far as we do but presents an analysis helpful as far as he goes. Germain Grisez and Joseph M. Boyle, Jr., *Life and Death with Liberty and Justice: A Contribution to the Euthanasia Debate* (Notre Dame and London: University of Notre Dame Press, 1979), pp. 336–441, lays out and applies to life-and-death issues the ideas treated in the present work, especially in chapter thirteen and fourteen.

A more historical treatment of the problem of chapter fourteen is Germain Grisez, "Toward a Consistent Natural-Law Ethics of Killing," *American Journal of Jurisprudence and Legal Philosophy*, vol. 15 (1970), pp. 64–96. R. A. Wasserstrom, ed., *War and Morality* (Belmont, California: Wadsworth, 1970), essays on war from various viewpoints.

Chapter fifteen will be supplemented by Eliseo Vivas, *The Moral Life and the Ethical Life* (Chicago: U. of Chicago Press, 1950), pp. 185–267, who treats the person as constituted by free commitment to objective values. Abraham H. Maslow, *Toward a Psychology of Being*, 2nd ed. (New York: Van Nostrand Reinhold Co., 1968), pp. 149–185, gives a psychological account of establishing self-identity that parallels our ethical account; note his treatment of values as objective potentialities. Erik Erikson, *Insight and Responsibility* (New York: W. W. Norton, 1964), pp. 83–134, another psychological account close to our view; his wholeness/totality distinction corresponds to our inclusivity/exclusivity distinction.

Chapter sixteen owes something to G. C. de Menasce, *The Dynamics of Morality* (New York: Sheed & Ward, 1961), a remarkable effort to show how human goods provide sufficient reason to be good. Our educational theory is closest to that of Montessori; see E. M. Standing, *Maria Montessori: Her Life and Work* (New York and Toronto: New American Library, 1962), esp. chapter 17, for an introduction.

Chapter seventeen on progress draws upon, but departs from, Charles van Doren, *The Idea of Progress* (New York: Praeger, 1967), which has a survey of theories of progress.

John Passmore, *The Perfectibility of Man* (New York: Charles Scribners' Sons, 1970), offers a full critique of moral progress theories; we do not consider him always fair to religious views. Herbert Spencer, *Illustrations of Universal Progress* (New York: Appleton, 1889), illustrates evolutionary optimism. A sympathetic presentation of Marxist views is John Somerville, *The Philosophy of Marxism: An Exposition* (New York: Random House, 1967), pp. 121–159.

Chapter eighteen may be supplemented by Michael Walzer, *Obligation: Essays on Disobedience, War, and Citizenship* (Cambridge, Mass.: Harvard U. Press, 1970), who discusses problems of revolution and reform, and related issues, in an ethical context based on the concept of social responsibility as communitarian. Norman Cohn, *The Pursuit of the Millennium* (New York: Harper & Row, 1961), pp. 307–319, sums up the implications of history for the idea that revolution is a panacea. Hannah Arendt, *The Origins of Totalitarianism* (New York: Meridian, 1958), pp. 460–479, develops the idea of ideology in relation to efforts to transform man radically. Lewis A. Feuer, *The Conflict of Generations: The Character and Significance of Student Movements* (New York and London: Basic Books, 1969), offers a historical and psychological study of student movements, suggesting much of their energy is wasted. H. L. A. Hart, *The Concept of Law* (Oxford: Clarendon Press, 1961) and Lon L. Fuller, *The Morality of Law,* rev. ed. (New Haven and London: Yale U. Press, 1969) present philosophies of law based on contrasting ideas of the national community. The two authors think they disagree, but Hart's theory emphasizes the contract aspect of civil society while Fuller's theory attends to its community aspect; the two together give a fairly adequate understanding of what law is. Grisez and Boyle, *Life and Death with Liberty and Justice,* especially chapters two, ten and thirteen, deal with certain questions of philosophy of law. John M. Finnis of Oxford University has written a major, comprehensive work in philosophy of law, making use of the ethical theory articulated in the present work: *Natural Law and Natural Rights* (Oxford: Clarendon Press, 1980).

Chapter nineteen's reference to Nietzsche can be illustrated in Friedrich Nietzsche, *The Portable Nietzsche,* ed. Walter Kaufmann (New York: Viking, 1954), pp. 197–200. E. H. Madden and P. H. Hare, *Evil and the Concept of God* (Springfield, Ill.: Thomas, 1968), state and develop the objections based on evil. Germain Grisez, *Beyond the New Theism: A Philosophy of Religion* (Notre Dame and London: University of Notre Dame Press, 1975), provides (pp. 274–324) a tight, technical treatment of the existential objections to the existence of God and religion; this work articulates the metaphysical foundations of the ethics we present here. Gabriel Marcel, *Homo Viator: Introduction to a Metaphysic of Hope* (New York: Harper & Row, 1965), pp. 29–67, develops the concept of hope. Vincent Punzo, *Reflective Naturalism: An Introduction to Moral Philosophy* (New York: Macmillan, 1969), pp. 315–368, deals with ethical objections to religion and suggests a role for religion in moral life similar to our hope. Bertocci and Millard, *Personality and the Good,* pp. 677–697, present a somewhat similar view; Punzo is Catholic; Bertocci and Millard are not.

Chapter twenty's reference to Sartre can be verified in Jean-Paul Sartre, *Being and Nothingness: An Essay on Phenomenological Ontology,* trans. Hazel E. Barnes (New York: Philosophical Library, 1956), pp. 464–481. Dietrich von Hildebrand, *Christian Ethics* (New York: David McKay, 1953), pp. 161–166 and 453–463, deals with religious commitment as basic in life.

Index

229

John Polkinghorne has had a distinguished career as a particle physicist and as an author of books exploring themes in science and religion. He was elected a Fellow of the Royal Society in 1974 and was Professor of Mathematical Physics at the University of Cambridge in 1968–79. In 1982 he was ordained as a priest in the Anglican Church. Since 1989, John Polkinghorne has been the President of Queens' College, Cambridge. His books include *The Particle Play* (W. H. Freeman, 1979), *The Quantum World* (Longman, 1984), and *Science and Christian Belief* (SPCK, 1994).

Science is very successful in discovering the structure and history of the physical world. However, there is more to be told of the encounter with reality, including the nature of scientific inquiry itself, than can be gained from impersonal experience and experimental test alone. *Beyond Science* considers the human context in which science operates and pursues that wider understanding which we all seek. It looks to issues of meaning and value, intrinsic to scientific practice but excluded from science's consideration by its own self-denying ordinance. The author raises the question of the significance of the deep mathematical intelligibility of the physical world and its anthropically fruitful history. He considers how we may find responsible ways to use the power that science places in human hands. Science is portrayed as an activity of individuals, pursued within a convivial and truth-seeking community.

This book neither overvalues science (as if it were the only worthwhile source of knowledge) nor devalues it (as if it were to be treated with suspicion or not taken seriously). Rather *Beyond Science* provides a considered and balanced account that firmly asserts science's place in human culture, maintained in mutually illuminating relationships with other aspects of that culture.

Also of interest in popular science

The Thread of Life: the story of genes and genetic engineering
SUSAN ALDRIDGE

Remarkable Discoveries
FRANK ASHALL

Evolving the Mind: on the nature of matter and the origin of consciousness
A. G. CAIRNS-SMITH

Prisons of Light – black holes
KITTY FERGUSON

Extraterrestrial Intelligence
JEAN HEIDMANN

Hard to Swallow: a brief history of food
RICHARD LACEY

An Inventor in the Garden of Eden
ERIC LAITHWAITE

The Clock of Ages: why we age – how we age – winding back the clock
JOHN J. MEDINA

Improving Nature? The science and ethics of engineering
MICHAEL J. REISS AND ROGER STRAUGHAN